Whitman's
Ride Through Savage Lands

with

Sketches of Indian Life

O. W. Nixon, M.D., LL.D.

Author of "How Marcus Whitman Saved Oregon." "The Mountain Meadows," Etc.

Introduction by
James G. K. McClure, D.D., LL.D.

Profusely Illustrated

Published by
The Winona Publishing Company
1905

COPYRIGHT, 1905, BY
THE WINONA PUBLISHING COMPANY

OLIVER WOODSON NIXON. M. D., LL. D.

PREFACE

I RESPOND with pleasure to the invitation to write a series of sketches of pioneer missionary history of early Oregon for young people. Its romantic beginnings, of the Indian's demand for "the white man's book of heaven," and especially to mark the heroic act of one who, in obedience to a power higher than man, made the most perilous journey through savage lands recorded in history. The same leading facts of history I have before used in my larger work, "How Marcus Whitman Saved Oregon." In this I have simplified the story by omitting all discussions with critics and historians, stated only as much of historic conditions as would make clear the surroundings, and have interwoven with all, real incidents from wilderness and savage life. They are not only the experiences of the heroic characters, but some of my own when the West was wild more than a half a century ago.

O. W. N.

Biloxi, Miss., January, 1905.

INTRODUCTION

N O. character in Sir Walter Scott's tales appeals more directly to my heart than "Old Mortality." He had a high and noble mission, to make live again the old-time worthies, and to keep in remembrance the brave deeds of the past. Any man who follows in his footsteps, and makes the world see in vivid light the heroes of another day, is to me a public benefactor. When, then, Dr. Nixon writes of "Whitman's Ride Through Savage Lands," and shows the force, wisdom, and unselfishness of Dr. Marcus Whitman and his accomplished wife, I feel like doing everything within my power to express my gratitude and to secure the reading of his book.

The tale, as he tells it, is very interesting. It is a tale that has been often in the mind of the American public of late years, but it cannot be too often told nor too often pondered. It has in it the very elements that nurture bravery and patriotism. Dr. Nixon tells it well. In simple, straightforward language he gives us the whole story of Dr. Whitman's life-career, indicating the forces that inspired him and the results that attended his efforts. Dr. Nixon sees in the events of the story the guiding and determining hand of Providence. With a wisdom justified by the needs of the ordinary human mind he calls attention to the part God himself had in the career of his hero, and thus he gives to his story an uplifting significance which a thoughtless reader might fail to note.

It is the glory of our American life that every part of our land has its splendid heroes. The Atlantic and Pacific coasts are one in having been the scenes where courage and devotion have expressed themselves. The earlier years of our national history brought into recognition the deeds of greatness done in the East. These later years are being used to make manifest the endurance and manliness that marked so much of settlement and progress in the West. Plymouth deserves its monument to the Pilgrims. So does Walla Walla deserve its monument to Dr. Marcus Whitman. From boundary to boundary of our wide domain we have had heroes, the stories of whose lives tend to make devotion to duty and allegiance to God transcendently beautiful.

Among such stories this of Dr. Whitman has high place. The personality of the author of it comes often to the front in his pages, but none too often. His own experiences serve to heighten the effect of the story, and give deeper impression to the facts narrated.

I look forward to the influence of this book with pleasure. I see boys and girls rising from the reading of it with clearer views of self-sacrifice, and with a more determined purpose to make their lives daring for the good.

The book carries with it a conviction of the worth of the best things, that is most healthy. It teaches important lessons concerning missionary helpfulness, that the reader accepts without being aware of the author's purpose.

A nation to have the lion's heart must be fed on lion's food. The story of Dr. Whitman is such food as may well nourish the lion heart in all youth, and develop in our American homes the noblest and most attractive Christian virtues.

JAMES G. K. McCLURE.

LAKE FOREST, ILLINOIS.

CONTENTS

CHAPTER I

CHAPTER II

CHAPTER III

CHAPTER IV

CHAPTER IX

CHAPTER X

CHAPTER XI

LIST OF ILLUSTRATIONS

CHAPTER I

The Lewis and Clark Centenary Exposition in Port-
land. The Great Captains. Their Guides, Hoe
Noo Chee and Sacajawea (The Bird-Woman).

A GREAT Exposition of the arts and indus-
tries of the whole wide world is to be held
this summer in the beautiful city of Portland, Oregon. It is to commemorate the grand
achievement of a few brave men and one brave
woman, who lived, labored, and conquered a century ago. At the call of their commander, they
exiled themselves from home and friends; they
crossed the wide deserts, climbed through gorges
and peaks of the "great Stony Mountains," strug-
gled through the pathless forests of giant firs, lived
among wild beasts, and wilder men, until they
reached the pathless Pacific Ocean—that was then
but a waste of water, where great whales sported
and the seals found abundance of food amid rocky
shores and islands for safe homes. Now teeming
multitudes inhabit the fertile plains; through the
rugged mountains pass the great highways of the
world—along the charted coast are many ports,
where white-winged fleets lie at anchor and the

great black freighters load and unload the commerce
of many lands.   But Portland still retains many of
the old landmarks.   The beautiful Columbia River
still flows by it to the sea, forests are not far away,
and "the everlasting hills" are about it, with their
white-capped peaks piercing the sky.

A hundred years ago, a vast and unknown
wilderness stretched from the Mississippi to the
Pacific Ocean—it was a land of mystery of unknown extent.   Millions of wild cattle that we call
buffaloes roamed over its plains, wild beasts hid away
in its mountain fastnesses, the beavers and otters
built their homes along its rivers, and wild tribes
of savage men made pitiless war upon each other,
though not destitute of many noble traits of character.   The young republic of United States had
far more territory east of the Mississippi than they
could manage or protect, so gave small care or
thought to what lay beyond.   But one thing they
had learned, that, for their own safety from foreign
aggression, and the protection of their commerce,
they must gain possession and control of the great
river.   Thomas Jefferson, that wise and far-seeing
statesman whose name and fame grow as the years
go on, was President at that memorable time of
great opportunities, and through his influence with
Congress induced them to make the great Louisiana
purchase, which gave to our government the South-

ern and Gulf states, the control of the Mississippi
River, and, as Jefferson believed and claimed, the
whole country to the Pacific Ocean. He had,
perhaps, but little knowledge of its vastness or its
value, but it has been said that his friend, the great
naturalist Audubon, who wandered up and down
the world searching out its wonders and beauties,
had told him many things about the great western
country. So he again appealed to Congress for an
appropriation to send out an expedition to learn
something of the nature and value of their new
possessions. The pitiful sum of two thousand five
hundred dollars was allowed. Captains Lewis and
Clark of the United States army were selected to
lead the expedition, and with them were sent a
botanist, a geologist, an engineer, and some soldiers,
who were required each to make a full report of
their journey, which took three years to accomplish. It is significant of the indifference of the
government in the matter that these reports were
sent to Washington and were laid aside for several
years when—through Jefferson's influence again—
the captains' reports were handed over to Richard
Biddle of Philadelphia, who made a brief abstract
of them, constituting one small volume, that passed
for many years as an account of the Lewis and
Clark exploration, and it has not been until within
the past three years that any genuine copy of these

reports has ever been published. It is small
wonder then that thirty years later Oregon remained
an almost unknown and unclaimed country.   The
young captains and their company, full of enthusiasm for their work, made their preparations and
purchased their supplies, mostly at their own ex-
pense, and left the last marks of civilization at
St. Louis in the spring of 1804.

The heroic little company made its first
winter camp at Fort Mandan on the Upper
Missouri, ready for an early start in the spring.
The success of the expedition in a strange land
through the long line of savage tribes was dependent largely upon a good guide and interpreter.   Lewis and Clark had secured Toussaint
Chabonneau, a Frenchman, who had renounced
civilized life, married, and settled among the
Indians.   He had traveled over wide stretches of
country, and had a small knowledge of the language
of several tribes.   Sacajawea, the wife of Chabonneau, was a handsome Indian girl of seventeen years.
She had been captured by the Minitaree Indians
when a small child, from the Shoshone Indians far
up in the Rocky Mountain region, held by them as
a slave, and sold to the Frenchman who made her
his wife.   Sacajawea was delighted with the prospect of again journeying toward her old home, but
continued to do the menial work for the company,

SACAJAWEA (THE BIRD-WOMAN).
Guide of the Lewis & Clark Expedition.

as is customary for Indian women.   Captains Lewis
and Clark, before many weeks upon their journey, saw that their real guide and interpreter was
not Chabonneau, but Sacajawea, his wife.   Their
way along the great river proved the identical
route which the captive child had taken from her
home into slavery, and with Indian nature and
sagacity, every notable spot remained in her
memory.   She told them of the streams in advance
that flowed into the great river, and the tribes
through which they were to pass; she told them
her history; she was the daughter of the great
chief of the Shoshone Indians, who were rich in
land and horses.   They owned large possessions
reaching to the foot of the Rockies, to which they
came during the summer months.   It was there
where she became a prisoner.   When they reached
the place she ran like a child and pointed out the
spot in the bushes where she hid to escape her
enemies.

Captain Lewis said: "Our hope now is to
find these Shoshones and their horses.   Here
we must leave our boats and prepare for mountain and land travel."   Sacajawea explained the
habits of her tribe the best she could, but it was a
vast wilderness by which the company was surrounded.   Both Captains Lewis and Clark with
their best men scoured the country, and finally

succeeded in finding the Shoshones, who had fled from their supposed enemies. They were led before the great chief Cameahowait. There they told of Sacajawea as best they could, which at once aroused attention. The chief ordered horses and provisions, and with many friends of the lost princess they went with Captain Lewis and his men to camp. Sacajawea recognized her brother, now head chief of the tribe, and as well the playmates of her childhood, and with tears in her eyes, and dancing with joy, she embraced them. The talk was long, for the Indian girl had to learn the fate of her family and friends. Had she desired she might have remained and resumed an easy life with her tribe.

Nothing now was too good for the white men, for they were brothers and friends. Sacajawea was their interpreter, and they received everything they needed for comfort, such as provisions and horses, for the journey to the Pacific and the return.

In meeting the many savage tribes and asking favors and permission to travel in safety through their domains, it was not the flag nor the guns they carried, but Sacajawea with the papoose upon her back and her wise diplomacy that opened the way and made them welcome. Upon the home journey the little Indian girl rode ahead with the captains, having richly earned her honors and the love

of all.   When the journey came to an end, Captains
Lewis and Clark begged that Sacajawea and her
husband accompany them to Washington, but
Chabonneau preferred the wild life he had chosen,
and the brave little woman dropped from civilized
history.

Well may the women of beautiful Oregon in the
coming Centennial take an honest pride in com-
memoration of the deeds of Sacajawea.   It is most
appropriate that the beautiful bronze to be then
erected to her memory has been designed and exe-
cuted by an American woman, Miss Alice Cooper,
of Denver.

We copy these stanzas of a poem by Bert Hoff-
man, who epitomizes admirably the reasons for
Sacajawea's honored place in this Centennial history:

Sacajawea.

"The wreath of Triumph give to her;
    She led the conquering captains West;
She charted first the trails that led
    The hosts across yon mountain crest!
Barefoot she toiled the forest paths,
    Where now the course of Empire speeds;
Can you forget, loved Western land,
    The glory of her deathless deeds?

"In yonder city, glory crowned,
    Where art will vie with art to keep
The memories of those heroes green—
    The flush of conscious pride should leap

To see her fair memorial stand
   Among the honored names that be—
Her face toward the sunset, still—
   Her finger lifted toward the sea!

"Beside you on Fame's pedestal,
   Be hers the glorious fate to stand—
Bronzed, barefoot, yet a patron saint,
   The keys of empire in her hand!
The mountain gates that closed to you
   Swung open, as she led the way,—
So let her lead that hero host
   When comes their glad memorial day!"

The heroic explorers of a century ago richly earned the honors they are now to receive, and wherever and whenever the names of Lewis and Clark are spoken or written in honor there also should be the name of Sacajawea, the Indian girl of the wilderness.

Thus the crowning success of the great expedition which gave the United States its second strong legal claim to the whole grand Oregon country was shared by the brave, true, diplomatic Sacajawea ("the bird-woman"). Readers of the complete story to follow will not need to be reminded that the heroes and heroines who thirty years later braved danger and death to save beautiful Oregon to the Union were only making sure the grand work thus inaugurated.

In course of time vessels on voyages of discovery drifted around Cape Horn, sailed up the long coast line of the Americas, always searching for that which would bring them wealth. Finding the immense quantities of furs gathered by Indians in the Oregon country, both the Americans and the English established trading-posts on the coast. The great Astor fortune that still remains in the family had its origin there. But the English had more money, more men, and more ships than the Americans, and before many years they ruled alone and the great "Hudson Bay Company" ruled the land. They established trading-posts eastward, and fleets of vessels carried the rich spoils of forest and ocean to all the countries of the world. At the time of the beginning of our story Dr. John McLoughlin was chief factor of the "Hudson Bay Company" and virtual king of the country. He was a noble old Scotchman, who had married an Indian wife to whom he was loyal and true all his life. He was kind and just to red men as well as white, and always ready to hold out a helping hand to all who came to him. But he served the English government and was always careful that no rivalry to the company he served should be allowed in the territory they claimed.

CHAPTER II

*The Visit of the Flathead Indian Chiefs to St. Louis.
Was the Story Authentic? Incidents—the Banquet Speech—Sketches of Indian Life and Character. Hoo Goo Ahu and Sacajawea.*

IT was a beautiful morning in the closing days
of October, 1831. The trees about St. Louis
were robed in their gorgeous autumnal foliage.
High above came the "honk, honk, honk" of the
wild geese, as in long, straight lines or in letter V's,
they winged their way southward, while the birds
were gathering in groups, chattering and arranging
for their winter outing in warmer lands. The resi-
dents of the city were just arousing from their sleep,
smoke was beginning to curl above the chim-
neys, shutters and doors were being opened for
business activities, when the strange scene was
presented of four Flathead Indian Chiefs, march-
ing solemnly single file down the middle of one of the
principal streets. At that date the now prosper-
ous and great city of St. Louis was but a "frontier town," mainly noted as a military station, and
Indians were not uncommon, as all the great and

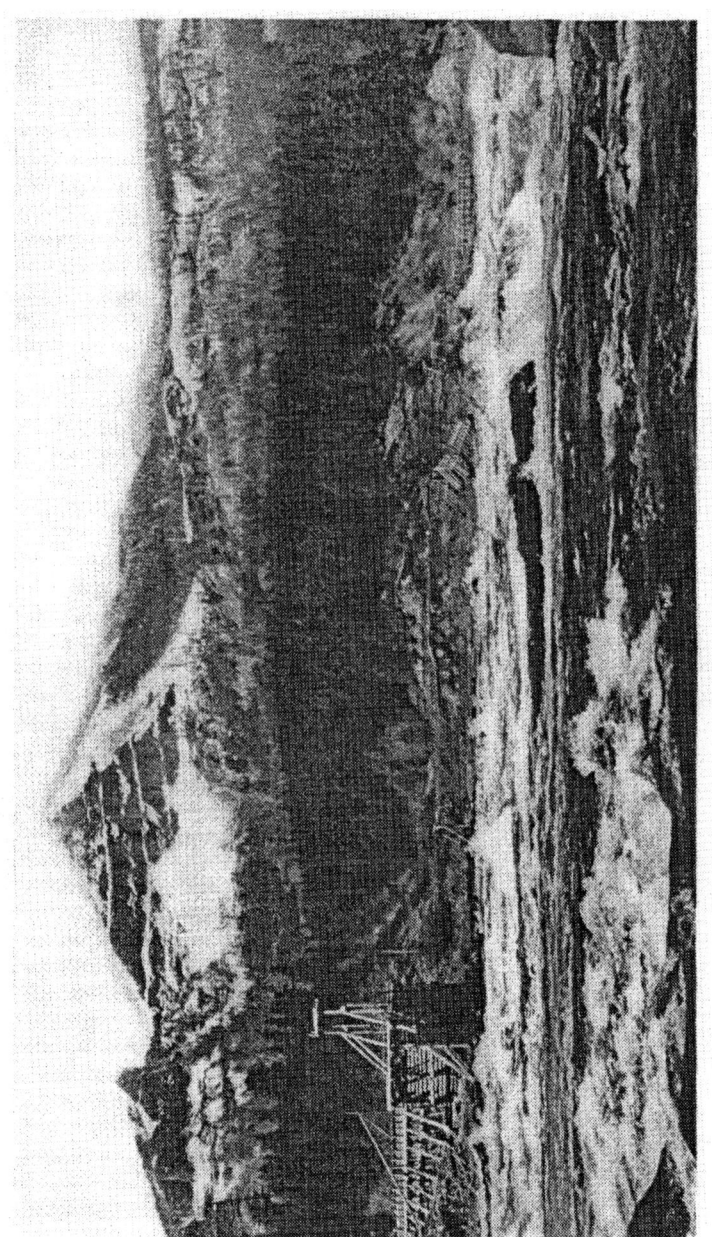

CASCADES OF THE COLUMBIA. (B. H. Gifford, photo)

fertile country north and west was occupied by them. But these were new and unusual in appearance, and attracted attention. Their bare heads in front were as flat as boards, and their long hair was interwoven with eagle quills; their dress and dignified bearing all indicated notable men from some far-distant tribe that the people had not before seen.

General George Rogers Clark, then in command of the department, was promptly notified of the visit of the strangers, and sent two of his aids to escort them to the barracks, where they could be comfortably lodged and fed. It is a singular historical fact that General Clark, in command at St. Louis in 1831 and 1832, was "the great red-head chief," as the Indians called him, who, with Captain Lewis, made the exploration of the Oregon country in 1804–1806, an exploration which for romance and completeness of its success has never been equaled in American history. General Clark in that expedition received marked kindness and aid from the Nez Perces and the Flathead Indians. He knew them in their homes, in eastern Oregon, and had a keen remembrance of their savage hospitality to him in his time of need. A band of the Flatheads also owned a large territory south of the Columbia and east from Astoria, and not far from the winter camp of the explorers. The author found them there, and spent a day with them in one of their villages in 1850.

General Clark had been in many hard Indian fights, and was of a family of famous Indian fighters, but he learned in that far western expedition to respect the hospitality, the courage, the heroism, and manliness of the Indian. He resolved to leave nothing undone to express his gratitude to his old Oregon friends, and he charged his young men to see to it personally that they had every comfort. He knew Indian character and stoicism, and when his aids told him they "could make nothing out of the Indians, or learn what they wanted," he replied, "Don't hurry them, give them time, and they will make known their mission to this far-away place." General Clark was an earnest and devoted Catholic, and he ordered that the Indians be taken to all the services in the cathedral, and also to all places of amusement likely to entertain them. Week after week passed, and the Indian stoicism continued; but finally in an audience with the General they told him all. The Indians all spoke "the Chinook," a pleasing word language invented by the Hudson Bay Company, and was to all the Indian tribes, from Hudson's Bay to the Columbia, what the classic languages are to the learned world. It was their trading language.

The General had a good interpreter, and knew

something of the Chinook himself, so that he soon fully understood the meaning of their long journey, and wondered at it.   They said, ''Our people have heard of the white man's book of heaven, and we have been sent the long journey over mountains and wide rivers, and among strange people, to find it and carry it back with us.''

In that far-away period there were few newspapers in the West, to print the news, and General Clark, with his many duties and cares, left no written account of these interviews or of his advice to the Indians, but we can rest assured that, as a soldier, a friend, and Christian gentleman, it was the most kindly he could give.

During the winter, as it was thought at the time, either from exposure in the long journey, or from the rich food to which they were not accustomed, two of the old chiefs died, and were given honored soldier burials.   The first to die was the memorable ''Black Eagle,'' recalled to-day by the Nez Perces as ''Speaking Eagle.''   He was an aged man, greatly loved by his people.   The records of the old St. Louis Cathedral have the account of Black Eagle's death and burial.   The second death followed soon after.   It proved latterly that this was the beginning of that terrible scourge, Asiatic cholera, which spread, in 1832, over a wide section.   Mrs. Clark, who kindly ministered to the Indians with her own hands, was "stricken with a malady that no physician could master, and died." As the spring approached, the two surviving chiefs began preparation to return to their distant homes, and General Clark left nothing undone to outfit them with every comfort for the journey. The steamer Yellowstone was just then loading for her first trip up the Missouri River, and he engaged berths for the two chiefs—the boat was to run as far up the river as it could go with safety—and would save the Indians many long, weary marches.

In addition to their necessary outfit, they had received numerous presents for themselves and friends at home, they greatly prized, to which Chief Min refers in his banquet speech, in the words, "You make my feet heavy with gifts." The night before their departure General Clark gave them a banquet, to which all his officers and many leading citizens were invited. Upon that occasion Chief H. C. O. Hcotes Min (no horns on his head), at the request of the General, made a speech in the Chinook language.

The Speech

"I came to you over the trail of many moons, from the setting sun. You were the friends of my fathers, who have all gone the long way. I came with an eye partly open for my people who sit in darkness. I go back with both eyes closed.

How can I go back blind to my blind people? I made my way to you with strong arms through many enemies and strange lands that I might carry back much to them. I go back with both arms broken and empty! Two fathers came with us; they were the braves of many winters and wars. We leave them asleep here by your great water and wigwams. They were tired in many moons, and their moccasins wore out.

"My people sent me to get the White Man's Book of Heaven. You took me to where you allow your women to dance, as we do not ours; and the book was not there! You took me to where they worship the Great Spirit with candles, and the Book was not there! You showed me images of the Great Spirit and pictures of the Good Land beyond, but the Book was not among them to tell me the way. I am going back the long trail to my people in the dark land. You make my feet heavy with gifts, and my moccasins will grow old in carrying them, and yet the Book is not among them! When I tell my poor blind people, after one more snow, in the big Council, that I did not bring the Book, no word will be spoken by our old men or by our young braves. One by one they will rise up and go out in silence. My people will die in darkness, and they will go on a long path to other hunting-grounds. No white man will go with them, and no White Man's Book to make the way plain. I have no more words."

Translated into English, doubtless the charm of the speech has been marred, and loses much of its terse and simple beauty. Those who doubt and sneer about a savage making such a speech do not know Indians. I have listened to Indian orators, and been charmed by their ease, eloquence, and wonderfully electrifying power, amid rugged surroundings. Indians have their orators and story-tellers, and are as proud of them as ever cultivated people are of their Beechers, Phillipses, Douglases, and Depews; and their animal stories far excel those of "Uncle Remus." In long evenings under the summer skies, or winters by the wigwam fire, they gather, and listen spellbound to the weird stories—wild, visionary, and superstitious—of the present life, and of the happy hunting-ground to which all are urged to aspire.

The Indian is a spiritualist, not an idolater. The medicine man is the great man of the tribe. When an Indian feels the call of the Spirit to become a medicine man, he goes off alone to the forest or to the mountains, or to some noted healing spring, fasts, prays, and seeks there for his power, through all the agencies of nature that surround him. Like Joan of Arc, he "hears voices" in the trees and from the rocks, the winds, the waters, the animals, and the birds. When he returns to his tribe and convinces the braves that he has received the Spirit, from that day he is entirely trusted. The greatest chief must consult him concerning every movement; whether it be the distant chase, change of location, or of war. He is Sir Oracle.

The writer does not speak at random or by hearsay of Indian life. He saw and studied something of it, more than half a century ago, before civilization had wrought the changes now seen. Indians

STRANGE VISITORS IN OLD ST. LOUIS.

are profound believers in the immortality of the soul.   Some suspend their dead in the leafy tree-tops, that they may the more easily ascend to "the happy hunting-grounds."   The custom of many is to kill the favorite horse and bury it with all accoutrements and implements of war, as well as their finest garments, believing the spirit will need them and receive greater honor.   The leading thought of the Indian seems to be that all material things have a spirit that is immortal.   The Indian burying-grounds are sacred spots and seldom if ever are desecrated in savage life, even by their worst enemies.   Some of the beautiful little islands in the rivers of the Far West have thus been used, as the many ruins testify.   It has long been noted that Indians in war will risk their own lives to carry off and bury their dead and prevent mutilation of bodies.

Is the Story of the Flathead Chiefs of 1831–32 Authentic?

So strange and so without precedent in savage life was the mission of the Indians to St. Louis, that many have doubted the truthfulness of the report, and have called it "visionary."   Fortunately the reader need not be in doubt in regard to the entire truthfulness of the event as reported. The Christian people of that time believed and acted upon it in a way to convince every honest mind of their earnestness. It may be said the incident made a profound impression in the religious world, and the history we are to recite of the after-results mark it as one of the providential events guiding the nation by unseen hands to its destiny.

Had such a notable event occurred in modern days, it would have entered at once into current literature. That it did not at the time is no disparagement of its truthfulness. There is one strong chain of evidence regarding the mission of the Nez Perces chiefs, not easily broken; that is, the written evidence of George Catlin. Aboard the steamer Yellowstone, upon which General Clark sent his savage friends, there happened to be a celebrated artist, George Catlin, then on one of his visits to the West to paint Indian pictures and study Indian life. These Nez Perces chiefs at once attracted him, and they became intimate friends—during the long journey he made pictures of them. Indians are not great talkers, and he did not learn much from them as to the object of their long journey. From others afterward he heard of their strange mission to St. Louis, and believing he had secured two historic pictures, he first wrote General Clark, and afterward met him, and was assured by him that such was the mission of

the four Flathead chiefs. Catlin, in his Smithsonian report for eight years, in 1885, says:

"These two men, when I painted them, were in beautiful
Sioux dresses, which had been presented them in a talk with the
Sioux, who treated them very kindly, while passing through the
Sioux country. These two were part of a delegation that came
across the Rocky Mountains to St. Louis a few years ago to
inquire for the truth of a representation which they said some
white man had made among them, that the white man's religion
was better than theirs, and that they would all be lost if they
did not embrace it. Two of the old and venerable men of the
party died in St. Louis, and I traveled two thousand miles,
companions with those two fellows, toward their own country,
and became much pleased with their manners and dispositions.
When I first heard the report of the object of their mission, I
could scarcely believe it, but upon conversing with General
Clark, on a future occasion, I was fully convinced of the fact."

The two pictures are now numbered 207 and
208 in the Smithsonian Institution, and highly
prized. H. H. Hcotes Min (no horns on his
head), who made the notable banquet speech, died
near the Yellowstone River on the journey home,
and but one, the youngest of the four, Hee-Ah-
K. S. Te Kin (the rabbit skin leggins), lived to
reach his tribe beyond the Rockies. As was customary with the Indians, a large band was sent
along the trail far away to the Rocky Mountains to
meet the expected delegation of chiefs with "the
book of heaven." Their legends say, "Rabbit
Skin Leggins shouted when far off, 'A man will
be sent with the book.'" The world of to-day

may well give thanks, that both Christian men and women were "sent with the Book" at that earnest and honest appeal. Christianity is broad, and its command is to "preach the Gospel to every creature." The Nez Perces Indians, who, in blind faith, sent for teachers, were blessed in the act above all Indian tribes in the land, and the blessing has followed them from that day to this. In another connection in a later chapter will be read facts in proof of their condition, and showing the effect of the Gospel verses upon Indians. Indian men, like the whites, are made up of good and bad. The missionaries were bright, shrewd men and women, and they easily saw that so fair a land could not much longer be held by savages in its unfruitful condition. They bent themselves to the heavy tasks laid upon them, to do the best they could for their savage wards. The true story for our pages, however, does not take us into any large study of missionary work, but mainly along the lines of Christian patriotism.

The author in answer to any critics of the missionaries to the Indians will relate a simple incident in his own experience, which dates fourteen years after their advent in Oregon. It shows how the seeds of Christianity they planted made of savages unselfish and humane men. It was on a Saturday, after days of weary traveling, we came to a little valley where we at once resolved to rest for a couple of days.   It was such a little paradise that we named it "The Valley of Blessing."   On Sunday morning, with a single companion, the writer wandered for miles up the narrow valley, enjoying its luxurious surroundings.   To the right was a mountain whose rugged sides were covered with dwarf firs and cedars; while rocks were piled on rocks looking like ancient castles in ruins.   Flowering vines climbed to the tops of the trees, and their fragrance filled the air.   A clear stream divided the valley where flocked myriads of birds from the mountain, as they drank and bathed, whistled cheerily to their fellows in the mountain home.   As we were admiring all this wilderness of beauty, on rising a little eminence, we came suddenly in view of four Indians, digging at a short distance away. We immediately dropped behind the hill, but not before we had been observed by the Indians.   We were watchful and well armed, but the old Indian gave us a peace signal, and we approached the spot. The company was made up of an aged Indian, eighty or more, his grandson, and two half-breeds. They were digging a grave and were silent as we stood until its completion.   The old Indian then invited us to look at the corpse under the shade of a near-by tree.   We were astonished to find it the emaciated body of a white man.   It was wrapped in a well-tanned buffalo skin, white and clean. The four Indians took the body and placed it in the grave, and the old man, removing his cap, to our astonishment, said, "Now, maybe some white man who knows religion will make a little prayer over the poor fellow!" The half-breeds, perhaps not understanding the English the old chief spoke, began pushing in the sand with their moccasined feet. Thus the Argonaut of 1850 was laid to his final rest, with only the wild birds to sing his requiem. The old Indian had brought along a smooth board to place at the head of the grave, and at his request, 1 wrote:

John Wilson, St. Louis, Mo., 1850.
Left by his company and nursed by Hoo Goo Chee.

He told us Wilson had traveled as long as he was able, and begged his companions to leave him there alone to die. He told the chief he had no complaint to make of his fellows. We mention the incident to show that the beautiful trait of unselfishness has a place even among Indians. The old chief could easily have buried the body near his mountain home without bearing it the long distance to be near the road, where the grave could be seen by his friends. He might have used an old blanket instead of the costly dressed robe the Indian prized so highly. Here we found a savage who, like the Flatheads, had heard of "the white man's book of heaven,'' had practically caught its unselfishness and humanity, and its spirit of love.

It is well to remember that the Indian has no literature, and has ever been dependent upon his enemies to write his history and his achievements. They have chosen to write only of his savagery. This is not fair treatment by the United States government, incited by justice, and the wholesome Christian sentiments of the land has during the past thirty years done much to correct all abuses of its savage wards.

CHAPTER III

The Effect of the Banquet Speech. How it Stirred Christian People. The American Board Acts. Drs. Parker and Whitman Go on a Voyage of Discovery. His Indian Boys. His Marriage and Journey through Savage Lands to Oregon.

THE Indian oration at the St. Louis banquet was translated by a young man present, William Walker, who was an Indian chief, but a white man, and it was first published some months later in "The Christian Advocate" in New York, with a ringing editorial from its editor, Rev. Dr. Fiske, headed, "Who will Carry the Book of Life to the Indians of Oregon?"

The effect was electrical among religious people in the East. The Methodist Foreign Missionary Society were prompt to act, and the very next year sent two able-bodied, earnest Christian ministers, Jason and Daniel Lee, with one layman to aid them. They reached their field by the long, round-about waterway, via London and the Hawaiian Islands. For many years they did effective work, far up on the Willamette River. The American Board, then under the control of Congregational and Presbyterian churches, was more cautious. It was an unheard-of proposition to come from savage life so far away from civilization, and they wanted time to investigate. The Rev. Dr. Samuel Parker of Utica, New York, became restive under the delay, believing fully in the call of the Indians, and resolved to join some trading company to the Far West and go to Oregon. In 1834 he reached the border upon the Missouri, but the fur-traders had departed. He returned home and renewed his efforts to arouse the American Board to action. He found Marcus Whitman, M. D., as much of an enthusiast in the work as he, and the Board resolved to send the two men upon a voyage of discovery in 1835, and to have them return and report upon the possibility of establishing missions in that well-nigh unknown land. So in 1835, the minister and the young physician were on the western border in time to join a company of American fur-traders, bound for Green River, in what is now northern Utah. Upon reaching this point they met some two thousand Indians, representing various tribes living within five to seven hundred miles. There were large delegations of Oregon Indians to trade their furs for articles needed. When the object of the missionaries was explained to the Indians, they received the news with such enthusiasm as to dispel every doubt from the minds of the mission-

aries of the wisdom of their course and the Indians'
sincerity in asking for Christian teachers. Upon
consultation they agreed that it was wise to make
no delay in reporting to the American Board.
While Dr. Parker was to continue his journey to
Oregon with the Indians, Dr. Whitman was to
return with the convoy, make the report, and
return the next year with reinforcements to begin
mission work. The Indians showed such confidence in Dr. Whitman's promise to come to them
after one more snow, that they selected two of their
brightest, most intelligent, and muscular boys
about eighteen years to accompany him, and help
him on his way the coming year. Dr. Parker,
with his Indian guides, reached Oregon, over which
country he traveled extensively. He organized no
mission, but studied the situation fully, so as to be
able to make a wise report for the future guidance
of the American Board.

Finding a ship sailing next year for the Hawaiian
Islands he did not wait for Whitman and his company. Dr. Parker was a scholarly man and a keen
observer, and upon his return wrote a book of great
value. It was a true description of Indian life and
conditions, the wealth of forest and the prospective
finds of coal and minerals in the hills and mountains, the magnificence of rivers, the healthfulness
and mildness of the climate. The book passed

through six editions, and was interesting reading, but it was of a far-away land, and induced little or no immigration at that time.

Dr. Whitman and his two Indian boys joined the fur company for escort on its return trip. While on the plains a scourge of cholera broke out, and the Doctor's skill and his untiring work to save the lives of the men, won all their hearts, and they united in giving him a cordial invitation to join them in the spring, upon their annual visit to Green River. This was gladly accepted, as such an escort was a necessity in that day. The Doctor and his two Indian aids reached Rushville, New York, late on a Saturday night in November, 1835. His return was unexpected, and his first appearance to his friends was when he marched up the aisle of the church with his Indian boys, as they sang the opening hymn. His good old mother was so astonished that she spoke right out in meeting, "If there ain't Mark Whitman!" It is easy to conceive that such an incident called out a wide interest and inquiry, which was just what the Doctor desired, enthused as he was himself in the importance of the work before him. The Doctor had taken great pains all summer to instruct his Indian boys in English, and they proved apt pupils. He put them at once in school, where they made rapid progress, and were general favorites.

Never was the enthusiastic young Doctor more active than in the fall and winter months in making his preparations. The American Board had resolved to establish a mission in Oregon, and they notified him that they preferred to send married men into the missionary field. This was unexpected but welcome news to Whitman, and was in accordance with the last advice from Dr. Parker: "Bring with you a good wife." He had already in his own mind made his selection in the person of Miss Narcissa Prentice, a daughter of Judge Prentice, of Angelica, New York, but owing to the privations and perils of the journey, and the isolated life among savages, he had hesitated to ask her to make such sacrifice. One can easily imagine his happiness, when upon fully explaining all, he found her with a courage equal to his own, and an abounding enthusiasm for the prospective work. After a time the clear-headed men of the Board, doubtless guided by their clearer-headed wives, raised a point, and said, upon such an expedition, so full of care and responsibility and danger, it would not do to send a woman unless accompanied by another of her sex. Here was a new dilemma. Time was passing, and candidates for such perils were not plentiful. The day of the wedding was postponed, and Whitman endeavored to meet the requirements. He finally heard of

AN INDIAN WELCOME.

Dr. Spalding and his newly wedded wife, who were en route to the Osage Indian Mission. He learned their proposed route and set out to find them. Whether through chance or Providence, he succeeded. It was a cold day and a driving snow, when in his sleigh he sighted them ahead, after a long chase. When in hallooing distance he shouted, "Ship ahoy, you are wanted for Oregon!" Hearing the cheery, pleasant voice, they halted, Whitman driving his sleigh by the side of theirs, and he at once bounded into the subject of which he was full. Dr. Spalding proposed that they go to the hotel in the town just ahead, where they could talk the matter over without freezing. By a glowing fire Dr. Whitman retold the story of the Flatheads, about whom they had read; of his journey to the Far West to verify the facts, and the result, and of the two Indian boys ready to escort them to Oregon, where they would meet with an enthusiastic reception such as he and Dr. Parker had received on Green River. Whitman was often called "The Silent Man," but when aroused and enthused, he was an eloquent pleader. And with all at stake, as in this instance, he was doubtless at his best. They listened with profound attention. Mrs. Spalding was an educated woman, of great decision of character, an earnest "Christian," and a firm believer in a power higher than herself ready to guide her in life's duties. They were silent for a moment, when she arose and said, "I desire a few moments to myself for prayer," and retired to her room. The two men sat by the fire canvassing all the dangers of the expedition and the hopefulness of the outlook. Dr. Spalding afterward wrote, in speaking of the meeting, "I do not think she was gone from us more than ten minutes before she returned, her face all aglow with happiness and enthusiasm, and said, 'Yes, we will go to Oregon!'" He continues, "I gently expostulated, 'My dear, we must consider your health in such a hazardous undertaking.' She replied, in the words, 'Go ye into all the world and preach the Gospel to every creature, there is no exception made for ill health.' "And no words of mine could alter her determination." Mrs. Spalding had been a semi-invalid for months, but her faith and Christian courage were strong. It was her prompt decision which decided the fate of the Oregon mission, of the four notable characters, and we may add, the fate of questions so great and grave to the nation, as to be unfathomable by man's wisdom.

The wedding day was again fixed. In this case there was more than usual interest in the bride, for her friends all knew of her destination.

The late Mrs. H. P. Jackson, of Oberlin, Ohio, sister of the bride, has told me in letters, of the events of the pleasant occasion. The two Indian boys, dressed in their best, were guests of honor. Dr. Whitman introduced them to his wife, and says Mrs. Jackson, "When he told them she would go with them to their far-away home in Oregon, and teach them, they did not try to conceal their delight."

Narcissa Prentice was the eldest daughter of Judge Prentice, an influential, earnest Christian man, then residing in Angelica, New York. The daughter was well educated, loved for her womanly qualities and famed in all the country around for the sweetness of her voice. She was the leader of the church choir of the village, and the people crowded the building the evening before their departure to bid the little party a good by and give them a blessing. After a good social time, the minister, the Rev. Dr. Hull, called the meeting to order, and gave out the old familiar hymn:

> "Yes, my native land, I love thee,
>   All thy scenes I love them well;
> Friends, connections, happy country,
>   Can I bid you all farewell?"   Etc.

The late Martha J. Lamb, editor of the "Magazine of American History," who wrote the report of the farewell gathering, says:

"The great audience joined in singing the opening stanzas, but soon they began to drop out by ones and scores, and sobs were heard all over the audience. The last stanza was sung by one voice alone in a clear, sweet soprano, and not a faulty note; it was the voice of Narcissa Whitman."

It was the last time her old friends heard the sweet voice, for daylight found them braving the winter storm on their way to Oregon.

The late Eli G. Coe, of Illinois, then a young man, drove them in his sleigh to the mountains, en route to Pittsburg, where they were to take boat for St. Louis. He has given me ·a delightful sketch of the journey, upon which he marks Whitman "The Silent Man, ever thoughtful of all his guests," and Mrs. Whitman, "The lovely little woman who was the life of the company, who often dispelled gloom, and made all forget the winter cold, by a song of cheer."

Their route was from Pittsburg down the Ohio River to the Mississippi up to St. Louis, thence up the Missouri River to near where Fort Leavenworth now stands. The journey had no mishaps until they reached "The Big Muddy," as the Missouri has long been called. Those who navigated it half and three-quarters of a century ago, will never forget the journey. It was sand bars on sand bars, forever shifting with each freshet, and snags galore! The engineer stood constantly at his lever, to answer the bell, a leadsman stood

in the bow casting a lead and calling in loud, sing-
song the depth of water, until suddenly, like an
electric shock, came the sharp, "five feet scant,"
and the bell rang, and the wheels reversed with a
suddenness that aroused every one, until he got
used to it. They were hung on snags, "hard
aground" on sand bars, and as a consequence were
four or five days behind the time at Leavenworth.

The reader will recollect that the fur-traders had
given Dr. Whitman a cordial invitation to join
them in the spring, and he was impatient but helpless in the delay.   To the great discomfiture of the
missionaries upon reaching the landing, they learned
that the fur company had left four days before.
What added to Whitman's trouble was, that at St.
Louis he had been told he could get all the provisions he lacked at the fort, and upon inquiry, found
nearly everything sold, and that he would have to
start in poorly equipped with provisions, without
a hope of being able to add to his stock, except by
chance and courtesy of the traders.

This was the first great test of the courage of
Dr. Whitman.   Dr. Spalding was outspoken, "We
must turn back and never think of such madness
as to brave a journey among savages without an
escort."   Whitman said little, but rapidly made
his preparation, simply declaring, "We will go on."
Mrs. Spalding nobly seconded Whitman, and said,

"I have started for Oregon, and to Oregon I will go or leave my body upon the plains." Mrs. Whitman was alike cheerful. So soon as harness could be adjusted, the loads packed, and the cattle rounded up, the man of courage gave the order, and the little train began to move through the deep mud of the Missouri River bottoms. We learned after that the fur company waited one day over the stipulated time. But they had in some way learned at St. Louis that the Doctor was going to bring with him some American women for the journey, something never heard of before, and as they were expecting to have to fight their way at times, they did not care for such encumbrances, anxious as they were to have the services of the good Doctor. Thus it was a gloomy start for the brave little company. Dr. Whitman had made ample preparation for the comfort of the women in a spring-wagon, "the brides' wagon," fitted up with various little comforts and a protection in every storm. But it is doubtful whether two cultivated American brides before, or since, ever made so memorable a wedding journey. The party consisted of the two brides and their husbands, Dr. W. H. Gray, two teamsters, and the two Indian boys. We may add that somewhere in the Sioux country the boys picked up three other Nez Perces friends; one of them, Samuel, was added permanently to the company. Mrs. Whitman writes, "When the boys get together they make a great chattering."

They were in an Indian country from the first day's start, and met great numbers of savages, out on their hunts, many moving to new camps, and some on the war-path. At no time were the missionaries molested, but on the contrary, were treated with great courtesy, and as Mrs. Whitman wrote, "They seemed greatly surprised to see white women in the party." The Indian boys were soon in their element, and of inestimable value; they could swim the rivers like ducks, and took all the care of the loose stock, and were wise in the ways of plains' life. They could explain to any suspicious Indians the coming of "the great medicine men" they were taking to their people, and in a hundred ways were helpers to the little company. Mrs. Whitman, from the outset, rode on horseback with her husband, only occasionally resting in the wagon, and for company to Mrs. Spalding, who was yet an invalid.

We make no pretense of writing a continued narrative of the journey, but just enough to catch its spirit. We have seen in it a dreary and discouraged start, and none but a hero with heroines to encourage him would have entered upon it. They had now been a whole month on the way making forced marches, the trail of the fur-traders

getting fresher every day, until finally hearing
they were in camp on Loupe Fork, the wagons
pushed on and joined them.   The Doctor and Mrs.
Whitman were behind helping to hurry forward the
loose stock.   Finally, late at night, the Indian boys
begged the Doctor and his wife to ride on to camp
and leave them to drive the stock in at daylight.
But they refused to leave them.   Picketing their
horses out to graze, then with their saddles for
pillows, they lay upon the warm ground looking up
at the stars and slept.   At daylight they rode into
camp and were courteously received and praised as
"a plucky set."

The two American women, who had so alarmed
the old plainsmen as a burden and an en-
cumbrance, by their tact and kindness soon
won them as friends, and nothing was left undone
that the rough old fellows could do for their comfort.   They had succeeded so admirably in passing
safely for a month alone through the Indian country, that they began to have confidence in themselves.   But they learned that they had not yet
reached the point of real danger, and were glad to
be protected by such a stalwart troop.   The
Indians had a great respect for these pioneer traders, who were veterans of the plains and splendidly
armed.   The greatest anxiety was for the safety
of their stock at night, when picketed out to graze.

The Indians especially coveted the oxen and cows, which required careful guarding to prevent stampeding.   Cattle when frightened at night lose all sense, breaking away and running as long as they can stand, becoming easy prey for the savages, while horses and mules almost invariably break for the tents and wagons, and the company of men.

Camp at night is always made by driving the wagons in a circle, with tents pitched inside. The wagons make a protection from an enemy, and all their contents are in easy reach.

The year 1836 was a peaceable year among the Indians, and the buffalo and other game was so plentiful as to make small temptation for Indian depredation upon the white man's stock during this portion of the journey, but we may add they cast longing eyes at all times upon every good horse the white man rode.

In the Buffalo Country

The company had now reached the buffalo country, and soon began to see great herds containing thousands, and even tens of thousands.   Every spring the buffalo journeyed northward to the valleys and plains to feed on the rich grasses. It is a feast occasion, one of the greatest the Indian enjoys.   Tribes travel four and five hundred miles from their homes to meet the buffalo, and lay in a supply of dried meat, calf skins, and robes, and never forgetting to feast for a month while laying up winter stores. It is a novel and exhilarating sight to view the annual Indian migration to meet these noble wild cattle of the plains—the whole tribe, old and young, dogs and loose horses, with all their movable worldly goods brought with them packed on poles drawn by ponies. They settle down in the little valleys near springs, or along running waters, and arrange for work in advance with as much system as the farmer in the spring plows and sows. The buffalo country has generally, by mutual consent, been regarded as "peace grounds," but the desire for revenge has many times made it the scene of bloody contests and massacres. Hunting buffalo in those days, either by the Indians or white men, was not sport, but butchery. They were in such immense herds that, when running from their enemies, those in the rear could not get out of the way, and were an easy prey to any kind of weapon of death. The buffalo bull is the most gallant and noble among animals. On the march he leads, brings up the rear, and marches on the flanks, while all the cows and calves are kept in the center of the herd and protected from the bands of wolves, mountain-lions, and bears which linger around ready to devour the straying members of the herd. By a wonderful provision of nature, the buffalo calves are practically all of the same age, so that a herd in the long summer outing is not much detained upon its way, for the little one trots gayly beside its mother in a few hours. But while the little fellows are thus comparatively helpless, those who have witnessed the scene, bear testimony to the courage of the great, strong-necked, sharp-horned bulls who will attack a grizzly or a whole pack of wolves, or a mountain-lion regardless of his own danger. At such times he is even at night a sleepless, faithful picket ever on duty. He walks backward and forward along his picketed line like a trained soldier, and when the ground is wet, he treads a deep path in the sod, and the picket line of a sleeping herd can easily be traced long afterward, and often is referred to as "Indian trails." One would suppose that such nobility would command respect. But it never did. Even such explorers and writers as Parkman and his men never seem to have enjoyed the day unless, in addition to the calves they killed for food, they were able to tell of the slaughter of many "savage old bulls." At the time of which I write buffalo were seen by the million. Fourteen years later, when the writer visited the same region, they could be seen in single herds covering a thousand acres. When frightened and running, they were turned from their course with the greatest difficulty.

A train on the trail they were crossing was only safe in halting and allowing it to pass. The pressure from the rear was so great that the front could not halt. Some of the old plainsmen told of "a tenderfoot's" experience, who was going to have some "rare sport, and his pick of an entire bunch." He observed a large herd quietly grazing and saw by making a detour, up a dry ravine, where he would be hidden from view, he could get immediately in their front. He succeeded, and tying his mule behind him, concealed himself in the edge of some bushes upon the bank of the creek. He did not have long to wait, something in the rear frightened the herd and it began to come directly toward him. As soon as in reach, he began to fire and kill. It would break the ranks for an instant only, and he at once saw death impending, as there was not a tree large enough to climb. He had shot until his gun was hot, but all in vain. Just then his old mule tied in the bushes opened up his musical "honk, honk," such as only a thoroughly frightened mule can utter, and the whole herd opened right and left, and the man was saved.

Some have expressed a wonder that these noble animals, in such myriads, should so soon have disappeared. It is easily seen, in the fact of the improved firearms used by the Indians, and that they killed, for food, skins for clothing, and robes for the market, only the cows and calves. They selected only the choice cuts of the meat, and left the great bodies for the wolves and other varments. They could tan only the skins of cows and calves for clothing and for tepee covers. It was a sickening sight to pass over the place of slaughter, and thus see hundreds of bodies, with only tongues and choice cuts and skins taken. American hunters were equally sacrificial. Half a century later the writer rode over the same land and saw Indians, all across the region, with carts and pack ponies gathering up bones of the buffalo. Passing stations along the Great North- ern and Northern Pacific railroads, one passes ricks of bones half a mile long on each side, and as high as the tops of the cars, waiting for shipment East as fertilizers, and horn handles for knives and other uses in the arts. Only two living wild herds of buffalo are now reported, one small one in Texas, and one carefully protected by the govern- ment in Yellowstone Park. It would have been wise and humane had they been protected sooner by the strong arm of the law.

But it was the great good fortune to our missionaries to meet the buffalo herds. They started out poorly provided, and would soon have been in distress, for they had added three Nez Perces Indian boys to their company, and the

pure air and exercise upon the plains provokes
great appetites.   It was equally good for the fur-
traders, who had calculated upon the event.   So
the whole train stopped and began to kill and
"jerk" meat.   The Indian boys were in their element and veterans in the business, and laid in
bountiful supplies.   While it is fresh and juicy few
animals furnish more nutritious food.   A buffalo
porterhouse steak, cooked over coals at the end
of a forked stick, when the thermometer of appetite is up to "one hundred degrees in the shade,"
is a royal feast to be remembered.   If however
kept up long enough, the good old-fashioned pig
with lean and fat strips on his ribs, is quite a relief.
But the dried meat was the staple food of the little
company from that time on.   Mrs. Whitman cheer-
fully and jokingly writes in her diary, "We have
dried buffalo meat and tea for breakfast, and tea
and jerked buffalo for supper, but the Doctor has
a different way of cooking each piece to give variety to the entertainment."

Mrs. Whitman kept carefully a daily diary of
events of travel, which was luckily preserved, and
passed into the hands of her sister, Mrs. Jackson, of
Oberlin, Ohio, which I have been permitted to read
and from which have copious selections in my larger
work, "How Marcus Whitman Saved Oregon,"
after which it was passed on to the Whitman College

Library, where it is preserved as a precious treasure. The notable feature of this diary is its self-sacrificing spirit and good cheer. The scorching sun, the clouds of alkaline dust that stung the eyes and throat, the impure water they were compelled to use, the myriads of mosquitoes and buffalo gnats, all of which the author so well remembers as the dreariest things encountered in a long life, did not daunt the spirit of this delicate little woman. Not a word of complaint can be found in that daily diary, which was never written for the public eye, or for effect. The nearest to it was once, after being without flour or bread for weeks, she writes, "O for a few crusts of mother's bread; girls, don't waste the bread in the old home!" Men and women are all human, and I have no desire to picture my characters as perfect beings. They doubtless had their faults, but none who have not experienced some of the difficulties of that pioneer band, who, tired and worn with travel, sought sleep while hungry (after shaking out their blankets to be sure no snakes were within them), can censure. I repeat, it takes such experience to fully appreciate the heroism and unselfishness of such consecrated lives.

The old pioneers were wise geographers and surveyors. There were two things necessary for life upon the plains, viz., water and grass. They studied their maps and saw the Platte, North and South Forks, reaching northward and westward. So they made their trails along the banks, cutting off bends, avoiding impossible sloughs and hills, but keeping an eye upon the river in the distance, and ever working nearer to it when a detour had been made. The two Plattes thus furnish supplies for from five to six hundred miles. Travellers struck across the divide for the Sweetwater and its tributaries, until the foot of the Rockies is reached.

As the eyes of our travelers had rested for a month upon the snow-covered peaks of the great stony mountains, one can imagine it was a day of rejoicing when they began the ascent. The trail up "the South Pass" was so easy a grade that the horses and cattle scarcely felt the strain. One looking at it would surmise that this break in the great mountain was not an accident, but it was left for a great highway between the oceans, to make one family, and a United Nation. Striking mountains, after the long dreary summer upon the alkaline plains, hard as mountain-climbing is, was yet a change to be appreciated. I recollect distinctly, it turned our little company of sturdy men (a few years later) into rollicking boys who whooped and sang to get the echoes, and rolled great stones, until their arms ached, crushing down the mountain-side.

PACIFIC SPRING—JULY 4, 1835

A Notable Celebration

Here on the top of the Rockies, or just beyond the summit, is a spring appropriately named "The Pacific Spring," for its pure, ice-cold water bubbles up and in a silvery stream winds its way westward. It is a beauty spot as the author well remembers. A little valley upon the mountains, covered with grass and wild flowers, with grand views of valleys and mountains reaching farther away than the eye can follow. Here the missionaries halted and allowed the fur-traders to pass on. It was the Fourth Day of July, a day ever memorable in the mind of every patriotic American. True they were but missionaries, and far from home and friends, but they were home-lovers and patriots. So spreading their blankets upon the bunch grass, they brought out the American flag, unfurled it, and with prayer and song dedicated the fair land thence to the Pacific, to God and the Union. It was a prayer and song which after history proved a prophecy; and one in which the actors in this little celebration took so brave a part as to deserve their names enrolled among the nation's royal benefactors. God rules the world, and all history shows that he oftenest leaves the great and strong, and takes the weak and humble to accomplish his grand purposes. Eternity will reveal whether that dedication was one of the agencies which brought the after grand results. Certain it was, that it was the agency of Dr. Whitman and his heroism in carrying out that vow years after, and stirred up a spirit never before experienced, and aroused the nation to action.

No stage could have been grander for such a celebration. Behind were the long stretches of the great plains, and still beyond the civilization of the continent, the hope of the Christian world; while before was the wilderness in all its wildness, reaching to the Pacific.

The Rockies towered about them, glittering in the sunshine! The craggy peaks of the Wind River mountains loomed up in the north, with the Coast Range visible, like floating clouds in the far west. The luxurious grass, the towering pines, and flowers that perfumed the air, made the spot beautiful, while the history of the event is a fit theme for a grand national epic or painting. There have been many historic celebrations of the nation's birth, some upon battle-fields where victory perched upon the "the banner of beauty and glory," but none more impressive than when upon that mountain top, in 1836, Mrs. Whitman's musical voice echoed from the rocks and trees,

"The star-spangled banner in triumph shall wave,
O'er the land of the free, and the home of the brave."

They had now entered upon the scenic stage of their journey, and it was a delightful change from the dead levels of the plains.   They luxuriated in the pure ice-cold water, and magnificent scenery, but it was well for them that they knew none of the weary climbs ahead.   We will not pause to note events from thence to Green River.

There they met with exciting and interesting savage life in all its realities.   They found at "the rendezvous" two thousand Indians in camp, waiting for the coming of the traders.   A thousand or more were from the Oregon country, and among them friends and relatives of the Indian boys, who had come the long distance to meet and welcome them, as well as to trade.   They gave the boys a royal greeting, as they regarded them as heroes and great travelers.   They were proud of their accomplishments in speaking like the "Bostons," and when the missionaries vouched for their earnest, faithful services, the Indians were proud of their boys.   Here they stayed for nearly two weeks waiting for the completion of the trading.   The Indians regarded the missionaries as their guests, and taxed themselves to the utmost to amuse them by wild games and feats of horsemanship and mimic battles.   They scoured the hills and woods for game, brought fish from the river, and seemed to think even that not doing enough.   They at all times treated "the white squaws" with the greatest courtesy.   Mrs. Whitman marks this in her diary. She says:

"One of the chiefs brought his wife to our tent, and taking off his cap and bowing gracefully, introduced her as politely as any civilized man. Such encourages me to believe that much can be done for these poor people, and I long to be at work."

CHAPTER IV

*"Old Click-Click-Clackety-Clackety," the Historic
Wagon. Breaking Camps and its Incidents, and
the End of the Journey.*

BREAKING camp at Green River was a
noisy and gleeful occasion. Half-starved
Indian ponies, when they have rested a few
weeks, generally rebel when packs are cinched
with a "diamond hitch" around their well-marked
ribs. Upon this occasion amusement was diversified
and enjoyable, even to the actors. But both Indians
and traders were no novices in such business, and
soon the companies bade good by to each other and
started along the trails to their widely scattered
homes. It was the great exciting social event of
Indian life, this distant visit to trade. The Indians
there met friends and relatives, exchanged gossip,
gathered the few luxuries and necessaries of life for
the year to come. They brought with them squaws
and some of their children, and enjoyed their outing in their savage way as much as the élite do the
seashore or Saratoga, and judging of both, one
would say they had more fun. The Oregon
Indians were all anxious to be escorts to "the

Boston teachers." There were two intelligent traders from Oregon, Messrs. McKay and McLeod, who offered escort to the little company, which was gladly accepted, and they were of invaluable service in that most difficult portion of the journey. The faithful Indian boys, however, held their places of honor and trust to the last. Mrs. Spalding had for some time been on horseback, and enjoyed it more than the wagon, traversing the rocky roads. There was no longer need of two wagons, and one was left at the rendezvous; but "the brides' wagon" pulled out with the pack-train. My young readers may think it an uninteresting object to write about, but they must remember it is "the brides' wagon," fitted up with all the little accommodations for the first two white women who braved the dangerous journey across the great stony mountains to the Pacific. True, it was battered and worn, dust and mud and storms had robbed it of style. It is well for those who ride in palace cars and whizzing 'autos to remember the days of their great grandfathers and grandmothers, who, amid privations and perils, with the parting blessings of Puritan homes, pulled across the Alleghanies in rough wagons and hewed out homes, and built this great empire of the Middle West. The more often we remember the heroines of the past the more we will enjoy this grandest inheritance of the present ever left to any people. But there was more than sentiment to this wagon as we shall see later on.   It figuratively blazed the way, and "marked a wagon-road to the Columbia," and years after silenced the eloquence of America's greatest orator!

The battered old wagon was a source of amusement to the Indians, who rode in troops by its side to see the wheels go round, and hear its clatter. Especially was it a novelty to the younger Indians, who at once named it "Old Click-Click-Clackety-Clackety."   There was a plain wagon-road from the Missouri to Green River, and from thence to Fort Hall—there it stopped.   The royal owners of Oregon had long before prophesied and decreed, "there would never be a wagon-road to the Columbia!"   They did not want one.

The company reached Fort Hall safely, which was an outpost of the English Company, and only a pack trail led westward to the Columbia.   Captain Grant, in command of the post, knew his business, and that was never to allow a wagon to go beyond Fort Hall.   He at once told the company of the dangers and perils of the journey, of the impracticability of hauling a wagon.   If tried it would so detain them that they would be caught in the snows upon the mountains and perish.   His earnestness and arguments were such that he convinced most of them, who favored abandoning the wagon. Even Mrs. Whitman joined others in the entreaty to Dr. Whitman to leave the wagon and move on. "The Silent Man" said little, but went on with his preparations, and when the pack-train moved out, "Old Click-Click-Clackety-Clackety" clacked in the rear as usual. The real facts are, that Captain Grant had scarcely overstated the dangers and difficulties of the undertaking. From the day they left Fort Hall until the memorable baptism of the wagon in Snake River, the old wagon is one of the constant themes of Mrs. Whitman's diary. We read, "Husband had a tedious time with the wagon to-day. It got stuck in a creek and he had to wade to get it out. After that in going up the mountain the wagon upset twice." She describes the steep up and down mountain trails where at times the mules had to be unhitched and the wagon lowered with ropes (as the writer a few years later was compelled to do). She adds, "I wondered that the wagon was not turning somersaults all the time. It is not grateful to my feelings to see him wearing himself out with such fatigue. All the mountain part of the way he has walked in laborious attempts to take the wagon." About one week later Mrs. Whitman writes, gleefully, "The axletree of the wagon broke to-day. I was a little rejoiced, for we are in hopes it will now be left."

THE RUGGED TRAIL TO OREGON.

She adds, in her next note, ''Our rejoicing was in vain; they have made the wagon into a cart with the back wheels, and lashed the front wheels to the sides, determined to take it through in some shape or other.'' ''Worse yet'' (she writes a week later), ''The hills are so steep and rocky, husband thinks it best to lighten the load as much as possible, and haul nothing but the wheels, leaving the box and the trunk!'' What do you think of that, my girl readers? The brides' trunk, that came from the far-away home, with all its mementoes and tender memories to be sacrificed, and ''only the wheels'' taken! But the gallant McLeod solved the problem and ordered the trunk packed on one of his mules, and it made the journey safely, and the old wagon made into a cart, but its wheels and every iron sacredly preserved, was still a wagon; and under a power impressed upon one brave soul it moved on its great way, marking a wagon-road and a highway between the oceans. Those may smile who will, but they do not think deep, nor do they estimate how small and seemingly insignificant events shape the greatest events in a personal, and even national, life.

The last note of Mrs. Whitman's diary referring to the wagon says:

"August 13. We have just crossed the Snake River, the packs were removed from the ponies and placed on the tallest horses, while two of the highest were selected for Mrs. Spalding and me. Mr. McLeod gave me his and rode mine. The river is divided into three channels by islands, the last, a half a mile wide, and our direction was against the current, which made it hard for the horses, as the water was up to their sides. Husband had a difficult time with the cart, as both mules and cart upset in midstream, and the animals got tangled in the harness, and would have drowned but for the desperate struggle for their release. Two of the strongest horses were taken into the river and hitched to the cart, while two men swam behind and guided it safely to the shore."

There they were at Fort Boise, beyond the Snake, and in Oregon! The wagon-road was made! It was within easy reach of their future home. There it was decided to leave the cart until spring, together with half a dozen footsore cattle, which could be sent for, or exchanged for others at Fort Walla Walla. Packs were now divided and the patient mules, which had long drawn the cart, became packers.

An old wagon is the common rubbish in every farm-yard, and if my reader enters a protest to the large place I have given it, or to protest against Marcus Whitman for his persistent refusal to take the advice of his companions, I will state in simple defense, I believe Whitman was an inspired man! He never once made such claim, even to the wife he almost adored. Later on, as we shall see, he obeyed the same voice under far more trying cir-

cumstances, when called to make his midwinter
ride to save Oregon.

When his friends insisted in saying, "It is like
going down into the valley and shadow of death;
wait until spring," his only answer was, "I must
go now!" Who can fathom such mysteries in any
other way than that I have mentioned. The
chances are, he never dreamed of making a trail
for a great transcontinental traffic. It is not at all
likely that ever the thought came to him that he
should guide a great immigrant train over the same
route a few years later and the brides' wagon proved
a notable factor in his success.

The Last March

The incumbrances left behind, the company
moved on as rapidly as the loose stock could be
driven. It was still a wild, rugged road, but much.
of the country traversed was beautiful. They were
all now on horseback, and all their worldly possessions on pack-saddles. The weather was delightful,
game abundant, and there was now no danger of
starving, although they had long been without all
the luxuries common to civilization. But best of
all, they were buoyed up by the near completion of
a nearly seven months' journey of hardships and
danger. The day before they were to reach Fort

Walla Walla, the Doctor and Mrs. Whitman rode ahead of the company, and camped under the trees on the bank of the river, eight miles from the Fort. At daylight they were upon the road. Who can imagine the delight of the tired travelers, as they came in sight, at a distance, of human habitations and civilization! They spurred their horses into a gallop and rode to the gates of the Fort just as the occupants were sitting down to breakfast. The men and women of the Fort came at once and admitted them through the gates, and gave them a cordial welcome, and did their best to make them feel at ease.

Mrs. Whitman writes in her diary:

"September 1, 1836. We reached here this morning just as they were sitting down to breakfast. We were soon seated at table and treated to fresh salmon, potatoes, tea, bread, and butter; what a variety thought I. You cannot imagine what an appetite those rides in the mountain air give a person."

She playfully adds that,

"While at breakfast a rooster perched himself upon the doorstep, and crowed lustily. Whether it was in honor of the arrival of the first two white women, or as a general compliment to the company, I know not, but he pleased me."

The rest of the company reached the fort during the afternoon. Here they all were, and none missing, right upon the scene of their probable future labor.

The Cayuse Indians who had earnestly interceded for teachers were the owners of a great tract of fertile land on both sides of the Walla Walla River. Adjoining them, one hundred miles distant, was the Nez Perces, to whom all the missionaries felt indebted and attracted, because of the boy friends who had so faithfully served them during the long journey, and as well for their amiable dispositions. The Cayuse were smart Indians, whose wealth was in horses, which roamed over their rich pastures, and without care, kept fat the year through. But the Cayuse were not like the Nez Perces, always to be relied upon. They were sharp traders, and notably tricky. But our missionaries found they could do nothing by way of settlement until they presented their credentials and consulted with the ruling authorities—the English Hudson Bay Company at Vancouver, two hundred and fifty miles down the Columbia. They were urged to stop and rest before making the long journey, but so eager were they to get to their work, and to make preparations for the winter, that they declined the kind invitation. Large boats were secured, and strong-armed, experienced Indian rowers soon bore the party to their destination, through a land, and along rivers romantically interesting. They found great bands of Indians on their route, especially at the rapids, and The Dalles, where many found employment, as boats and goods had to be carried for miles to smooth water. Dr. Whitman at once marked The Dalles as an ideal place for a mission.*

Dr. McLoughlin, the chief factor of the Hudson Bay Company, received the party most cordially, and bade them welcome. He was known among the Indians as "The great white head chief." He was a giant in stature, a gentleman of culture and education, and a man with a soul as large as his body. From the outset there seemed to be a freemasonry attachment between Whitman and McLoughlin. They were much alike, physically and mentally. They were both physicians and men with high moral character, stamped in every act of their lives. McLoughlin carried out fixed principles in all his dealings with the Indians; he never allowed them cheated in any trade; he lived up to every promise made; and the savage tribes, in every quarter, obeyed his commands like good soldiers do their general. Whitman laid bare the whole case, how and why they were there, and concealed nothing. His ideas freely given were, that he believed savages must first be taught to build homes, plant and sow, and raise cattle, sheep, and stop their roaming life. This was directly what the Hudson Bay people did not want.

* Years after, and just before Dr. Whitman's death, he purchased the old Methodist Mission at The Dalles. His later judgment justified his first impressions.

They wanted furs and skins, and to get them whole tribes must each year migrate to the distant hunting and trapping regions. Dr. McLoughlin, while anxious to serve the missionaries, was yet true to his company. He had placed the Methodist missionaries Jason and Daniel Lee the year before far up the Willamette, and he explained to Dr. Whitman that The Dalles was not the place for a mission, and that it would be far better for the company and for the missionaries, to settle in a more distant quarter. It all resulted in Dr. Whitman going to the Cayuse on the Walla Walla, and Dr. Spalding to the Nez Perces, one hundred and twenty-five miles further on.

McLoughlin was so impressed with the honesty and earnestness of his guests, that he gave them liberty to draw upon him for anything he could furnish for their use and comfort. Such an unlooked-for kindness was greatly appreciated. And we may add, as far as Dr. McLoughlin could execute the promise, it was sacredly fulfilled. It is well to constantly remember that without his kindly aid the missionaries of Oregon would have suffered, or even starved. Having settled these important preliminaries, the little company was impatient to be at its work. McLoughlin saw the necessity of house-building in preparation for the winter, but protested against the wives leaving his roof until

homes were provided, and when he saw that
they hesitated and feared that they would tax
hospitality, he at once overcome all by stating it
would not overtax, but would be a great favor to
him if Mrs. Whitman would remain and give his
daughter lessons in music.   So it was arranged—
The husbands with helpers, tools, and seeds departed for the scene of their future homes.

The Cayuse Indians were delighted with the
arrangement, and at once set off six hundred and
forty acres of their best land at the junction of two
branches of the Walla Walla River for the mission.   Here the Doctor, his two teamsters, and
two he had hired set about house-building.
There were small trees all about the grounds and
along the river, but none suitable for lumber or
boards.   For all such they had to go from eight to
ten miles up the river to the foot of the Blue
Mountains, and saw by hand, or rive boards,
pack them on horses, or float them down the rapid
river.   It is easy to see that house-building was no
picnic job under such circumstances.   But Whitman was not an "eight-hour man," and he never
"struck."   He toiled early and late, and camped
down in the forest, and went to sleep with the
musical howl of the wolf in his ears.   The result
was, in less than six weeks there loomed up "a
commodious house," of one great room, with a

large open fireplace and nearly ready for guests.
It had a shingled roof, places for windows and
doors, and while the Doctor added the many little
conveniences for comfort, Dr. Spalding went to
Vancouver to escort the women, who were impatient, and anxious to be helpers of their husbands.
A house, whether a cabin or a palace, is never a
home until a good wife enters its doors. A man
alone can no more make a home home-like than
he can pack a trunk.

CHAPTER V

———

*The Home-coming. The Beginning of Missionary
Life. Clarissa, "the Little White Cayuse Queen."
Her Death. Sketches of Daily Events.*

AFTER a somewhat tedious journey up the
river for two hundred and fifty miles,
against the current and strong winds, Mrs.
Whitman and her escort reached the mission station
December 10th, and alighted from her horse at the
cabin door after dark, while the wolves from the
farther banks of the Walla Walla united in a vigorous howl, either of protest or of welcome. My girl
readers may imagine that the surroundings were
not such as would call out any enthusiasm in
a young wife, entering her first home. And yet
there is a beautiful lesson of contentment, thankfulness, and love shown in the words of this earnest
little Christian woman, surrounded by savage life.
She writes in her diary:

"We reached our new home December 10th, found a house
reared, and the lean-to inclosed, a good chimney and fireplace, and the floor laid, but no windows or doors, except
blankets. My heart truly leaped for joy as I alighted from my
horse, entered, and seated myself before a pleasant fire, for it
was night and the air chilly."

Again, December 26th, she writes (you will observe the date, one day after the world's greatest anniversary):

"Where are we now, and who are we, that we should be so blessed of the Lord? I can scarcely realize that we are thus comfortably fixed and keeping house, so soon after our marriage, when I consider what was before us."

Think of it, girls! no chairs except those rudely made with skins stretched across them. Table made of four posts, covered with boards sawed by hand; stools made of logs sawed of proper length; pegs along the walls upon which to hang the clothing, nails being too expensive a luxury to use. Beds were bunks fastened to the walls, and filled with dried grass and leaves, and yet the young bride, accustomed to the luxuries of civilization, set about building a home around which always cluster life's comforts and joys. Every page of her diary speaks her thankfulness for unnumbered blessings, and not a discordant note, or a complaint, or a regret in all the pages. If I were to stop to moralize, I should mark the love that only comes where gold glitters, as the demoralizing agency of our day in this Christian land. Young people desire too often to start in life rich, even when their honored parents toiled for years for life comforts. This desire for wealth is to-day so universal as to mark it the chief aim of life. To start rich and be happy have lured a multitude to misery. The little story I relate, however, tells its own moral in its simple facts, and needs few words to impress its beautiful lessons.

Mrs. Whitman thus describes the great farm and its surroundings. I have many times wandered over the old place, and cannot better describe it than to insert a note from her diary:

"It is a lovely situation. We are on a level peninsula formed by the two branches of the Walla Walla River. Our house stands on the southeast shore of the main river. To run a fence across, from river to river, will inclose three hundred acres of good land, and all directly under the eye. Just east of the house rises a range of low hills, covered with bunch grass almost as rich as oats, for the stock. The Indians have named the place 'Waiilatpui,' the place of the rye grass."

Upon one of the highest of those hills in the East, which Mrs. Whitman refers to, the pioneers of Oregon, Washington, and Idaho recently erected a stately marble monument to Whitman, and at its base is "the great grave" containing the remains of Dr. and Mrs. Whitman, and twelve others who perished in the massacre, which will be referred to more particularly in another chapter.

Dr. Whitman regarded it his first duty to plan to live in comfort, and set his Indians a good example. He toiled day and night in making his arrangements to plant and sow in the early spring months. The Indians flocked about the mission in great numbers, curious to see the active, earnest work of the man, and wondering at his accomplishments. Mrs. Whitman soon organized classes of Indian children, and entered with enthusiasm upon the work to which she had dedicated her life. Indian children are bright, docile, and quick-witted, and she soon had them under control, and saw rapid progress, considering the fact that each had to learn the language of the other at the start. The Cayuse were very anxious for their children to learn all the secrets of "great medicine" and often sat around the yard and grounds in groups to take mental note of events. Whitman tried hard, by example and otherwise, to persuade the Indians to lend a helping hand at work; now and then they would join him in some heavy lifting which one man could not do, but they did not believe that Indian men were made to work, that "work was only for squaws."

What Whitman accomplished may be best seen by a short extract from a book written by T. J. Farnham, who visited the mission in 1839, three years later. He writes:

"I found two hundred and fifty acres inclosed and two hundred acres under good cultivation. I found from forty to fifty Indian children in the school, and Mrs. Whitman an indefatigable instructor. One new building was in course of construction, and a small grist mill in running order. It appeared to me quite remarkable that the Doctor could have accomplished so much since 1836, and act as physician to the Indians, and also to the distant mission stations at Clearwater and Spokane. He could not have done so, and kept the mission work to its high standard, only by the tactful and unceasing work of Mrs. Whitman."

The Rev. Dr. Jonathan Edwards, writing of the mission, which he visited in 1842, says:

"I found the Indians had taken a practical lesson from the Doctor, and were each cultivating for themselves from one-fourth to four acres of ground, and they had seventy head of cattle and a few sheep."

The great crops of wheat, barley, potatoes, melons, and vegetables so easily raised in the rich soil were a revelation to the Indians, and taught them just the practical lessons the Doctor so much desired. His theory was, that little could be done in a religious way with the Indians until he could induce them to build homes, and plant and sow and reap, and adopt the methods of civilized people. Many had been induced to build houses, and much of the unnecessary nomadic life had been abandoned. Mrs. Whitman retained her wonderful voice and sang and won the hearts of the savages, long before she knew enough of the language to make the sentiment of her songs impressive lessons. From the outset she was regarded as their friend, and they embraced every opportunity, in their crude way, to show their appreciation. They often brought her presents of venison and wild fowl, which was an agreeable change of diet from the horse meat they were compelled to use for over three years. Their stock of cattle and sheep and hogs was too small to be used for food.

Mrs. Whitman says in her diary, in 1838: "To supply our men and many visitors we have this year bought of the Indians and eaten ten wild horses." Those young Cayuse horses that roamed over the rich pastures and nearly as wild as the deer, are not such bad food, as the author can testify. They are not to be compared with the old broken-down horses sometimes used for food by civilized people. Mrs. Whitman, in her diary, seldom enters a complaint against her Indian wards. She treated them as friends; nothing was kept under lock and key, and she declares nothing was ever stolen. But they liked to roam all over the house and were curious to see everything. After the home had been enlarged, as it had been each year, and bedrooms were added, she had a difficult task in teaching the Indian men that it was not proper for them to open the door or enter a lady's bedroom. They seemed to have difficulty in understanding that it was "a sacred place," and appeared hurt and aggrieved, lest that in some way they had lost favor with their good friend.

A Notable Event

Perhaps I should have noted it long before this, for it was a distinct event to these two people, so far separated from kindred and civilized friends, when a little girl baby came to cheer their rude home in the wilderness, seemed a gracious gift direct from paradise. To the Indians she was a wonder and delight. Great burly savages with their squaws came from miles and miles away to look upon the "little white squaw baby." They seemed to think it a great privilege and honor to be permitted to touch the soft, white cheek with a finger. To the sixty and seventy Indian children in the school, the baby was more interesting than their lessons, and the older and more careful Indian girls who were permitted to nurse and care for the little one during school hours were envied by all others.

In the pure health-giving air, with her vigorous constitution, the baby grew strong and vigorous. She was a precocious child physically and mentally, and before she was a year and a half old, she spoke both the English and Indian language. Her constant association with Indian children made her even more familiar with their language than the English. She had inherited a wonderful musical voice from her mother, and sang as the birds sing, because they cannot help singing.

MT. TACOMA FROM LONGMIRE SPRINGS. (The home of Nekahni.)

Later on, she incorporated Cayuse words in her songs which delighted the Indians, and they thought her almost more than human.   Every day they would lounge around the yard and watch every movement and listen to her songs.   The old chief was one of her great admirers; he called her "the little white Cayuse Queen," and openly gave notice that he would make her the heir to all his wealth, for he was rich, as the Indians understood riches. We have had but the meager facts, those written by Mrs. Whitman to her family and the notes in her diary, to guide us in telling the story of this fleeting beautiful young life.

An Impending Calamity

But an affliction was impending, even before the child reached two and a half years of age.   It was Sunday morning in June, and none brighter or more glorious than June days in Oregon, and the little girl had been permitted by her father as usual to select the hymn for the morning service.   The hymn was one unusual for the child of her tender years, but you must remember that at that far-away date there were few hymns adapted to children, and she selected one she had memorized.   It was the olden-time favorite

"Rock of Ages

"While I draw this fleeting breath,
When my eyelids close in death,
When I rise to worlds unknown,
And behold Thee on Thy throne;
Rock of Ages, cleft for me,
May I hide myself in Thee."

This was the morning family service; in the afternoon there was a large attendance of the Indians. The Doctor led the service, and for the opening hymn selected the same one sung in the morning, and the little girl's sweet childish voice chimed in beautifully with the rich soprano of her mother. Mrs. Whitman writes, "This was the last we ever heard her sing." I never hear "Rock of Ages," but it calls to mind little Clarissa, and her wilderness home, where the angelic messengers hovered even then, to bear the dear child, in the words of her song, "to worlds unknown."

After the service Mrs. Whitman was busy in the preparation of the evening meal for her large family; the little child was here and there, busy as usual, and had not been missed until five minutes before the alarm was given, and a hurried search made in every direction, with calls that were unanswered. They had a path which led to the Walla Walla River, sixty or more yards away, and a platform built out, so that pure water could be dipped up for family use. There upon the platform they found one of her little red tin cups, which was a treasure she greatly prized. The Indian who found it at once reached the conclusion that the little girl had fallen in while attempting to dip the water. He at once dived in, and allowing the rapid current to drift his body as it would the child, he soon seized the clothing and bore the little body, yet warm, to its father's arms. Every effort was made to recall the life which had departed, but in vain. Possibly my young readers may inquire why was this permitted? Why was the dear child taken, and such sorrow left in the home? Such thoughts and utterances have occurred thousands of times during the centuries. The pure, the good, and the true depart, and the vicious often live on. We indeed "look through a glass darkly" on this earth, but we may know more for the reasons of life when we reach the life beyond.

Certainly such events are trials of Christian faith in multitudes of Christian homes! Did they come too near worshiping the child? Was it likely the great, strong man who was to be called to a great work would have been turned aside from it had the child lived? Could the "Silent Man" have left that tender charge in the wilderness to answer a call to duty? Who can answer? Dr. Whitman himself writes nothing of the event. But one glancing at the notes of Mrs. Whitman's diary, will see revealed the profoundly Christian character of the mother. She writes, "Lord, it is right, it is right! She is not mine, but Thine! She was only lent to me to comfort me for a little season, and now, dear Saviour, Thou hast the best right to her. Thy will, not mine, be done!" One seldom reads a better sermon upon Christian faith than that.

The effect of the death of "the little white Cayuse Queen" upon the Indians was marked. They had but little of the faith of the mother's heart to buoy them up. They could not understand it. The Indians were superstitious, and they conceived it to be a judgment, sent by the Great Spirit, upon Dr. Whitman, and that he was displeased with "Great White Medicine." From that event the older Indians appear to have lost most of their interest in the mission and its work, and the task of the missionaries never after ran as smoothly as before. The best of them still attended the religious services, and the school flourished. The medicine men of the Cayuse had long been jealous of Whitman's power, and they helped the grumblers and mischief-makers to lessen the Doctor's power and influence with the tribe.

The occupants of the mission were very busy people. The fields and gardens produced bountiful crops, but it required it all to feed the many at the mission, and the hungry transient guests. It was upon the direct route of immigrants—many sick and impoverished, and they all met with hospitable welcome. Mrs. Whitman writes, in her diary, "In some respects we are in a trying situation, being missionaries and not traders." Dr. Spalding, who was more intimately associated with Whitman and his work than any other man, years after Whitman's death, made this record.

"Immigrants by the hundreds, and later on, and near the close of his life, by the thousands, reached his mission, weary, worn, hungry, sick, and often destitute, but he cared for them all. Seven small children of one family, by the death of parents, were left upon the hands of the Doctor and his wife, one a babe four months old. They adopted them with four others, furnishing food and clothing without pay. Frequently the Doctor would give away his entire food supply, and send to me for grain to get him through the winter."

The Cayuse Indians were scarcely a fair test of Dr. Whitman's theories of Indian elevation and civilization. They were smart, shrewd traders, and not fur-hunters, and a low state of morals existed. While many of the older ones accepted the Doctor's advice of living in peace with surrounding tribes and treating them honestly, yet many of the younger Indians rebelled against his strict rules, and went on forays that he severely condemned. In one case a distant tribe owed a debt which they had failed to pay, and the Cayuse braves made a foray and stole their horses to pay the debt. The Doctor made a vigorous protest, and the young bloods had to take back their booty, but it estranged many of the influential, younger Indians, who rebelled against such strict moral methods. Such conditions grew with the years. They were near the fort, and came oftener under the influence of the Canadian fur-traders and hangers-on of the Hudson Bay Company, and as we shall see later on, were easily led to believe the stories started at the time of the great ride, that "Whitman's designs were to kill off all the Indians, and take possession of their lands." But we will not enter into any discussion of the direct causes which led up to the great disaster of 1847, many of them not well authenticated.

The Nez Perces presided over by Dr. Spalding, whose mission was intimately associated with that of Whitman, and one in which he took a deep interest, was a much more tractable tribe, and have ever since proved their training. They are perhaps to-day as fine specimens of civilized Indians as can be found in the United States. From the year 1836, when Dr. and Mrs. Spalding took charge of them, they have never raised an arm or showed enmity against white people. One little faction led by a minor chief, at one time joined a

war party, which, however, was not countenanced
by the tribe. At the time of the great massacre,
when Dr. and Mrs. Spalding were also expecting
death, the Nez Perces rallied around them, and five
hundred of their bravest warriors escorted them
to civilization and safety, braving the scorn and
enmity of hostile tribes. To-day they are Christian
people, have five flourishing Presbyterian churches,
good schools, and productive farms. Every
fourth of July all the churches unite in "a yearly
meeting," raise American flags, hear speeches and
sermons, and patriotic songs. In the fine two-
volume history and biography of his father, General
Stevens, who was the first governor of Washington
Territory, Captain Hazard Stevens pays a noble
tribute to the work of the early missionaries and
the Nez Perces. He specifies as many as three
occasions when all the other tribes were on the war-
path, the Nez Perces stood loyal, and saved the
lives of the governor and his party. True, we
cannot, in view of the facts, have much to say of
the Cayuse, but they were not all bad. It was
related by those who visited the Cayuse in their
reservation, to which they were banished after
the massacre, that "fourteen years after, old
Istikus, every Sunday morning went to the door
of his tent and rang the old sacred mission bell,
and invited all to come to prayers." How little or

how much of Christianity was planted in Indian souls by the pioneer missionaries of Oregon eternity alone will reveal.

But we venture the assertion that the American Board and Christian people, in view of the good we know of the Indians such as I have recited, and the overwhelmingly invaluable services of Dr. Whitman to Christianity and the nation, no wiser expenditure was ever made by that great organization.

There is not a blight nor a blur upon the lives of the messengers of salvation who answered the Indian's call for "The White Man's Book of Heaven." They sacrificed ease and comfort and home and friends that they might brighten Indian life and point the way to the life to come. The strange thing about it all is, that the great multitude even of intelligent, Christian people have either never heard of or forgot to do them honor.

We must now turn for a brief retrospect of pioneer history relating to early Oregon. The author begs his young readers not to shun the chapter. It is important, for it is the key that unlocks the brave story to follow, of "Whitman's ride." It is good history to know, for it shows the stepping-stones of the nation's greatest progress.

CHAPTER VI

Brief Sketch of Discovery and History of Oregon Country. When Discovered! Who Owned It! By What Title! The Various Treaties, and Final Contest.

UPON the opening of the year 1792, the Oregon country was an unknown and unexplored land. It had been believed that a great river entered the Northern Pacific, and several nations had, from time to time, made investigations. It had been reported that ancient navigators had discovered it a century previous, but if so, it had no place upon any map. It was in that year that Captain Robert Gray, a merchant trader, whose ship was fitted out in Boston by a syndicate of merchants achieved the honor. Captain Gray was a native American, born in Tiverton, Rhode Island, in 1755, and died in Charleston, South Carolina, in 1800, eight years after his discovery. He was an observant sailor, as well as a Yankee trader, and as he was sailing leisurely in a gentle breeze, from forty to sixty miles from the shore, he observed a change in the color of the water, and upon testing it, found it comparatively fresh. He at once reached the conclusion that he had found the mysterious, long-sought river. Turning the bow of his vessel toward the shore, and keeping as near what appeared the middle of the fresh-water current, he, at first venture, entered the mouth of the river, and luckily one of its most easily navigated outlets (for it has several). He sailed up the river, anchored in its wide bay near where Astoria now stands, and raising the American flag, took possession in the name of the United States. He was impressed with the immense volume of water pouring into the ocean, and the grandeur of the great harbor, from six to ten miles wide, and the wild beauty of the new land. He sailed up and down the river, sounded its depths, traded his goods with savage tribes for furs and skins, got fresh supplies of pure water, fish, and venison. After a more than usual prolonged stay for a trading vessel, he again put out to sea, having named the great river after his staunch vessel, "The Columbia." *

It so happened that a week or more before making his great discovery he had spoken, at sea, to Captain Vancouver, of the English navy, who was upon a voyage of discovery on the Northern Pacific Coast. A few days after emerging from

*. . . . "He was the first,
That ever burst, into that silent sea."

the river he again came in hailing distance of the
English ship, and announced to Captain Vancouver
his great discovery, giving him all the bearings
which had been accurately taken.   Captain Vancouver immediately changed his course, found the
entrance, entered the river, sailed up the Willamette to its falls, up the Columbia to the rapids,
and formally took possession in the name of England!   It is a singular fact that both Spain and
England that year each had a ship along the coast
upon voyages of discovery.   We are accustomed
to call such events as "it so happened," but
whether accidental or providential, America was
ahead.   It will be well to keep these facts in mind,
for upon them hinges all claims England had upon
Oregon!   Yet, weak as they were, she held supreme
possession of all Oregon for nearly half a century,
and as we shall show, had it not been for the heroic
work of the old pioneer missionaries, would probably have held the whole fair land for all time to
come.   England owned the territory northward
from the United States, whose boundaries were not
accurately defined.   Even those along the borders
of the New England states were not definitely fixed,
and were a source of constant conflict until settled
by the Ashburton treaty as late as 1846.   The line
between the United States and Canada ran westward to the Rocky Mountains, and there ended.

Thirty-five years later, while England was in full
possession of Oregon, by a treaty signed in 1818,
to run for ten years (and was renewed in 1827 for
ten years more), her commissioners claimed that
they were "the owners of Oregon by discovery."
They argued that "Captain Gray only discovered
the mouth of the river, while Captain Vancouver
made full and complete discovery"; that "Captain
Gray's claim was limited to the mouth of the river,
and that he was only a merchant, sailor, and trader,
and not a legitimate discoverer, while Captain Vancouver was a commander in his Majesty's navy."

Mark, then, the discovery, in 1792, as the
United States' first claim to Oregon.   When the
United States purchased the claims of France to
all the great possession west of the Mississippi
River, it was supposed at the time to reach the
Pacific Ocean and include the Oregon country, and
was so marked on the maps until the publication of
the latest government map, which marks "The
Louisiana Purchase," reaching only to the Rockies.   So, by the after-light of history, we can make
no claim to Oregon from that purchase.   But
President Jefferson, who had a more enthusiastic
interest in the Oregon country than did any other
of the statesmen of his day, evidently believed his
purchase from France included the Oregon country, for he at once began to plan a voyage, for

survey and discovery, of all the lands from the Mississippi to the Pacific.

Jefferson looked much farther into the future grandeur of the nation than his fellows. While minister to France he met the great traveler and ornithologist, Audubon, and became deeply interested in the mysteries of the Western wilderness. He attempted upon his return to America, by private subscription, to send out an exploring expedition under the guidance of Audubon. But the death of the great naturalist defeated the enterprise.

Jefferson, in 1800, was elected President; he made the great Louisiana purchase; he believed it extended to the Pacific; and it was through him that the Lewis and Clark expedition was fitted out in 1804, and sent on its mission to explore the land. My young readers who desire the complete and thrilling story of the Lewis and Clark expedition can find it in "The Conquest," by Mrs. Eva Emory Dye of Oregon City.

The third claim for American ownership was the settlement at Astoria by the Astor Fur Company, in 1811. It had but a short life, as it was captured by the English early in the year of 1812, and not returned until after the final treaty of 1846.

Spain held an old fort on lands south of the Oregon country, really a shadowy and uncertain title. In 1818 a general treaty with Spain was signed in which she gave to the United States all claims she possessed in the Oregon country. This made the fourth claim to ownership. Mexico, which was a part of Spain at that time, in her northern possessions, laid claim to the same, and this was quieted by the treaty with Mexico in 1828. This made the fifth claim to ownership. It will thus be seen that the United States had but one competitor for title to Oregon, and that was Great Britain.

I have thus in the briefest way recited the important historical events relating to our title to the now valued country beyond "the great stony mountains." No facts of American history are stranger or more interesting, and the reader must catch the spirit of that period to find interest, and give due credit to the pioneers of that distant land for their grand work of rescuing it from a foreign power.

It is well to bear in mind that American statesmen, who in 1802–1803 arranged for the purchase of the territory west of the Mississippi River from France, had but two objects in view: one was to get possession of the mouth of the Missouri River, upon a demand made by the commerce of the western states; and the other was to get possession of the rich, alluvial bottoms of Louisiana for slave labor. It was those two elements combined which enabled President Jefferson to get the measure through Congress, in spite of the united opposition of New England, which was opposed to expansion. It is also a notable fact, worthy of remembrance, that sixty years later, all the great states carved out of the Louisiana Territory, except two, were solidly massed behind the flag and the Union to crush human slavery.

It reads like romance, but is true history, and caught in its spirit, shows an overruling Power dominating the nation's destiny.

The great Louisiana purchase not only failed to make slavery strong, but it eventually, and within half a century, was one of the strong agents for slavery's destruction.

CHAPTER VII

Why Did the United States Dicker with England for Half a Century, before Asserting her Rights to Oregon? The Answer—American Statesmen had no Appreciation of Oregon, and Determinedly Opposed Expansion.

IT is no pleasure for an American to call in question and criticise the wisdom and statesmanship of the men of the first half of the nineteenth century. But history is made of stubborn facts.

From 1792, the time of discovery of the Columbia River, up to 1845, the United States government never, by an official act in any way aided Oregon, or attempted to control it. Time and time again some statesman in Congress offered a resolution, or framed an act looking to that end, and upon several occasions one branch of Congress permitted the act to pass, simply to avoid discussion, knowing that it would fall dead in the other house. Thus, year by year our statesmen went on such record, as for their credit and wisdom it would be well if it could be obliterated from the records. They were men, brave and true; they

had guided the nation to an honorable place among
the nations of the earth, but they were, after all,
willing to stand still, and let well enough alone.
They regarded their territory as already vaster and
larger than would ever be peopled.   The readers
can best understand the canny sentiment of the
period by a few quotations from speeches made in
Congress from time to time when the Oregon question was brought before them.   Senator Winthrop
of Massachusetts, in one of his great speeches, said:

"What do we want with Oregon?   We will not need elbow
room for a thousand years."

Another senator, second to none in influence,
Benton of Missouri, in a speech, while in Congress
in 1825, said:

"The ridge of the Rocky Mountains may be named as a
convenient, natural, and everlasting boundary.   Along this
ridge the western limits of the Republic should be drawn, and
the statue of the fabled god Terminus should be erected upon
its highest peak, never to be thrown down."

In justice to Benton, we may observe he later
on was convinced of the unwisdom of the sentiment, and became, with his co-worker, Senator
Linn of Missouri, an ardent friend of Oregon.
But his colleague, Senator Winthrop of Massachusetts, as late as 1846, when the Oregon treaty was
before the Senate, and when the question had
reached almost a war stage, repeated the words of

Benton's speech of 1825, and commended it for its wisdom and statesmanship.

General Jackson, who was a power in the nation's counsels in that day, in a letter to President Monroe, concisely stated his opinion in these words:

"It should be our policy to concentrate our population, and confine our frontier to proper limits, until our country in those limits is filled with a dense population. It is denseness of population that gives strength and security to our frontier."

That was a diplomatic and conservative opinion, which doubtless reflected the sentiment of the multitude. The Calhouns, the Websters, the Daytons, and a host of others were more pronounced, and less diplomatic. They pointedly hated the very name of Oregon, and did not propose to endanger the nation's safety or defile its garments by making it a part of the Union.

To all that class, and I shall mention but few of them in illustration, Oregon was an aversion. The great Webster said:

"Oregon is a vast worthless area, a region of savages, wild beasts, deserts of shifting sands, cactus, and prairie dogs. What can we ever hope to do with a coast of three thousand miles, rock bound, cheerless, and not a harbor on it. What use have we for such a country?"

Senator McDuffie of South Carolina, was fiery with his oratory, and can easily be understood. He said in one of his several speeches:

"The whole of Oregon is not worth a pinch of snuff."

Again he said:

"As I understand it, there are seven hundred miles this side of the Rocky Mountains uninhabitable, where rain never falls, mountains wholly impassable except through gaps. What are you going to do in such a case? Can you apply steam? Have you estimated the cost of a railroad to the mouth of the Columbia? The wealth of the Indies would not build it. I wish the Rocky Mountains were an impassable barrier. If there was an embankment five feet high to be removed, I would not vote five dollars to remove it, and encourage our people to go there."

That speech was delivered in Congress only a few months before Whitman's memorable ride to save Oregon. Senator Dayton of New Jersey was marked as an able man, and yet his knowledge of Oregon was as limited as that of Webster, Winthrop, or McDuffie. In one of his speeches he called "Oregon a Sahara, except along the little streams and bottom lands!"

We have in modern times had some eloquent opponents to expansion, but they were "childlike and bland" when compared with the old statesmen of the first half of the nineteenth century, who easily saw ruin to the country by acknowledging practical ownership of that distant territory.

The public press was not behindhand with statesmen in ridiculing Oregon. The Louisville Journal and the National Intelligencer, then the two most influential newspapers in the land, were bitter. The Journal wrote, and the Intelligencer copied and approved:

"Of all the countries upon the face of the earth, Oregon is the one least favored by heaven. It is the riddlings of creation. It is almost as barren as Sahara, and quite as unhealthy as the Campana of Italy. Russia has her Siberia, and England her Botany Bay, and if the United States should ever need a country to which to banish her rogues and scoundrels, the utility of such a region as Oregon would be demonstrated. Until then, we are perfectly willing to leave this magnificent country to the Indians and trappers and buffalo-hunters that roam over its sand banks."

One passing over that beautiful and fertile land, after only half a century and ten years have passed, can easily conceive how dense was the ignorance of the common people upon the subject, when a man, eminent in letters, and the wisest journalist of his day, George D. Prentice, would give expression to such sentiments.

The English press if possible was even more pronounced, and used every argument to discourage emigration. The Hudson Bay Fur Company was owned and controlled by the titled nobility of England. It had made every owner rich by its wealth of furs. It was in full control of all the territory by the consent of the United States, and only desired "to be let alone" and in peace to enjoy the monopoly.

The London Examiner, in 1842, just when the United States was waking from its lethargy, wrote:

LAKE CHELAN—FIRST VIEW OF THE SNOWY PEAKS. (Photo., Lyman.)

"Ignorant Americans are disposed to quarrel over a country, the whole of which in dispute not being worth, to either party, twenty thousand pounds."

About the same time the Edinburgh Review wrote:

"Only a small portion of the land is capable of cultivation. It is a case where the American people have been misled, as to soil and climate. In a few years all that gave life to the country, both the hunter and his prey, will be extinct, and their places supplied by a thin half-breed population, scattered along the fertile valleys, who will gradually degenerate into a barbarism far more offensive than backwoodsmen."

In view of the utterances of the American press and statesmen, we remain silent in any criticism of England. It was acting no dishonorable part in Oregon. They were simply using to their great profit a vast territory the United States owned, but did not want to be troubled with. They, it is true, knew more of its worth than did Americans, but as far as the Hudson Bay people were concerned, they did not covet immigration, even of their own kind, only enough to hold the balance of power, and keep themselves in readiness to organize the territory, and retain it under terms of the treaty of 1818. They had great interests at stake.

Modern writers have asserted over and over again that "the United States was never in any danger of losing Oregon, and needed no Whitman and his missionaries to save it!" But they cannot do away with the record which I have only tersely recited.

A volume could be written, along the same line, to prove the utter lack of interest in that country. But if statesmen, in Congress and out, and the press had been silent, the single official act of the government, in signing the treaty of 1818, giving entire control of the land to England (for the Hudson Bay Company represented England), would tell the whole story of the neglect of Oregon. When ever before or since has the United States made such a deal, giving by solemn treaty, a country thirty times as large as Massachusetts, for a full twenty years and more, without a dollar of compensation, to a great foreign nation, and unresistingly seen American traders driven out or starved out of the entire country? Those making the charge of ''no danger of losing Oregon by the United States'' would do well to explain *this one act, which was official,* even if they make light of the utterances of the men who refused, for more than fifty years, to legislate by a single act for Oregon. It is true the treaty said:

"It should not be to the prejudice of either of the high contracting parties, the only object being to prevent disputes and differences among themselves!"

Who does not see and acknowledge that the treaty was a virtual acknowledgment of England's

ownership by "discovery" as claimed at that time?
These modern critics find no flaw in the title of the
United States, they simply shout "no danger" for
no other conceivable purpose than to attempt to
dishonor and disparage the heroic work of the missionaries and pioneers of early Oregon, in which
they have succeeded only too well. They were
poor men, who made no claim for honors. The
leading, heroic actor made no demands for his services, neither money nor official recognition. Our
historians, until modern justice cried out in shame,
have sought to bolster up the statesmen, lawmakers
and molders of public opinion of that day, only
giving sneers to a man who sacrificed ease, comfort, home and life to patriotic Christian duty.

CHAPTER VIII

The Conditions of Oregon in 1842. _The Arrival of
a Large Party of Americans._ _The News They
Bore._ _The Great Ride to Save Oregon._ _The
Incidents of Travel._ _Whitman Reaches Wash-
ington._

WE now reach a critical period in Oregon
history, and are to study events crowded
with exciting interest. Several new
missions had been organized by the American
Board, and were manned by a scholarly, heroic
band of missionary workers. They were Christian
men and women in the best sense of the term, and
were there in answer to the savage's appeal made
at St. Louis, to teach and read to them "the Book
of Heaven." But at the same time, they were
intensely patriotic American citizens. They had
been given passports by the United States
authorities before leaving the States; a copy of
that given Dr. Cushing Eells is still in the possession of his son, Myron Eells, now living in Washington. It varied, it is true, from regular passports,
but nevertheless was enough foreign to make its
possessor understand he was destined to "a foreign

land," and under the direction of "the Foreign Missionary Society."

The missionaries often met in conference, and generally at Waiilatpui, that being central, having larger accommodations than other posts.

Notwithstanding the courtesies and constant kindness personally received from Dr. McLoughlin, of the Hudson Bay Company, they were ill at ease. They had now been six years in Oregon, and realized its grand possibilities. Their bountiful crops of grains and fruits told them of the productive soil; the healthful climate, the great forests, the wild grand scenery, all emphasized its value. They were missionaries, far away from home, yet Americans, and patriots, to see so fair a domain year by year slipping away from the Union, ground them to the quick. In their private correspondence to friends, and Dr. Parker, in his able book, had encourged immigrants to brave the dangers of the journey.

The heroic Methodist missionary, Rev. Jason Lee, made a trip across the plains to Washington and brought back with him several Americans. Despite all their efforts, Canadians and adherents of the Hudson Bay Company outnumbered them three to one. The missionaries and all others in Oregon knew that the meaning of the treaty of 1818 was that, whichever nation settled the country

would hold and own it. They knew it had been
practically in possession of England for many years
with the direct sanction of American authorities. They knew the low esteem in which
Oregon was held by many American statesmen,
but what could they do? Such were the conditions
in 1842, when Elijah White, a former Indian agent
of the government, reached Whitman's mission in
the month of September. With him came one
hundred and twenty-five American immigrants.
He was an intelligent man, and had many in his
company who were thoroughly posted upon American affairs. They found Whitman an intensely
interested listener and questioner. In this company was a young lawyer, Amos L. Lovejoy, a
most intelligent man, who, in after years, filled a
large and honored place in Oregon history, and
latterly shared with our hero the daring and danger
of his great work.

What was before Congress

These men informed the Doctor that "the Ashburton treaty," fixing the boundary line between
the United States and Canada, which had run up
against the Rocky Mountain and rested there for
half a century, was under discussion between the
two governments, and would probably come before

the United States Senate for final action during the session of 1842–1843.

Whitman was a man of few words, and quick action. He pondered deeply. He felt that a climax was impending, and in the contest Oregon was to be lost or won for his country. I do not stop to argue whether it was simply the call of patriotism of the man as an American, or whether, like the men of old, "he was called of God," but when we remember the perils to be met, the sacrifices to be made, and none knew them better than Whitman, I cannot believe that so clear-headed a man would ever have entertained the idea, if he had not heard and obeyed a call higher and more commanding than that of man!

He laid the matter before his wife, his chief counselor, that he fondly loved and cherished. The two were as one. They had met dangers and hardships, sacrifices and sorrows, together for seven years. This meant separation and dangers unknown to both for a whole year, during which not a line or a word could pass between them to tell of the fate of the other. Words would fail to express or picture that September conference in the wilds of Oregon if it had ever been written. But Narcissa Whitman was the same heroic woman who years before sacrificed the ease of civilized life and rode on horseback across the dreary plains, climbed

mountains, and swam rivers, endured hunger at the
call of duty! She was an ideal missionary, and
the patriotic wife of a missionary who, in song and
prayer, had dedicated the whole fair land to God
and the Union upon that memorable anniversary
upon the Rockies in 1836, and she answered,
"Go!"

The Doctor at once sent messengers to the
several missionary stations, summoning them to an
immediate council at Waiilatpui for important business. They all responded promptly, glad to come
in contact with the many new guests from the
States, and hear words from home, as well as to
learn the meaning of this sudden and unusual call
for conference. Of this meeting, and what was
said and done, we have more complete reports,
from the written words of Dr. Eells, Dr. Spalding,
and other members. When assembled Dr. Whitman lost no time in explaining his call, and that it
was to obtain leave of absence from the local conference for one year, to visit Washington and the
States! The proposition was astounding to his
brethren, and caused wide discussion. While they
were, in the main, in full sympathy with Whitman,
they well knew the prejudices of the rulers of the
American Board against ministers "dabbling in
politics," or concerning themselves with questions
of state. A second important question was dis-

cussed, viz.: "If it became known to the ruling powers in Oregon, upon which all the missions were wholly dependent, would it not greatly embarrass if not destroy them all?" They had the kindliest feeling for Dr. McLoughlin for his eminent services rendered, but they well knew the Hudson Bay Company was there for business, and that it had starved out every American trader who had intruded upon their domain, even the wealthy John Jacob Astor was permitted only one year in Oregon, although he came with the direct sanction of the American government. The company owned all the ships which came and went each year to Hawaii and London, bearing their letters and bringing all the supplies they received from civilization. Would the good Dr. McLoughlin under such conditions be able to shield and protect them? (Further along it will appear that he did, and was driven from his great office for his aid to the missionaries.)

A third reason given was the immensity of the danger of such a journey in mid-winter—was like, as one expressed it, "Going down into the valley and shadow of death to attempt it."

A fourth objection was that while the local board was the adviser in regard to all local affairs of the missions, the home board at Boston required a permit officially signed for any missionary to separate himself from his work. All these questions were canvassed pro and con. The men of that conference were as brothers joined in the one great work, and the counsels given were free and earnest.

Dr. Whitman was mainly a silent listener. When the dangers of his trip were pointed out, and he was asked to "wait until spring," his sententious reply was, "I must go now!" In reply to the objection that he would violate the rules of the Board, Dr. Eells says:

"Dr. Whitman was so fixed in his purpose that he declared he would make the attempt even if he had to withdraw from the mission, remarking, 'I am not expatriated by becoming a missionary.'"

Continuing, says Dr. Eells:

"The idea of his withdrawal could not be entertained. Therefore, to retain him in the mission, a vote to approve his making the perilous journey prevailed."

There has been a contention made by persons ignorant of the facts, that "the sole purpose of Whitman's ride was to save his mission from being closed." It is a silly charge, and unworthy of refutation, except to state the facts. The immigrants in Oregon were curious to know the cause of such a journey, and the people of the Hudson Bay Company doubtless made inquiry, but it was enough for them all to know that "Whitman had business with the American Board," and let it go at that. The missionaries were under no obligations to make known facts detrimental to all their interests, and when the proper time came, all the actors told the whole truth in regard to it. The silence of the missionaries, which was imperative for their own safety, doubtless misled many. Whitman's object was definite and clear.

Dr. Spalding, explaining years after, says:

"The last words Whitman spoke to me as he mounted his horse for the long journey, were: 'My life is of little worth if I can save this country to the American people."

The time fixed for his departure by the Board was October 5th, and all set about writing voluminous letters, for it was seldom they had such opportunity. There was much talk and counsel as to a companion and helper of the Doctor on his way. A score of his trusted Indians would have been glad of the opportunity.

The Doctor pondered over the matter, and made up his mind, and approached General Lovejoy, and explained to him the urgency of the case that compelled him to go, and asked the blunt question, "Will you go with me?" He was delighted with the prompt response, "Yes!"

Mrs. Whitman was delighted that "a Christian gentleman like General Lovejoy would bear her husband company, and he would not be left alone

to Indians and guides on the long and dreary way.''
All was now hurry and preparation, and the few
things the good wife could find from her stores
were gathered and packed.   On the 2d of October,
for a double purpose of visiting a sick man and
securing some needed stores, the Doctor rode to
the fort, and while there heard news of an incoming colony of immigrants from Canada.   As he
galloped home to the mission, he saw increasing
danger, and resolved there should be no delay.

It was a great occasion, that beautiful October
morning at Waiilatpui.   A number of Indians
were to go with the party to make sure they got
on the new trail to Fort Hall, much shorter and
easier than that traversed by the missionaries in
1836.

There were a large number of immigrants
around Waiilatpui, and they with many Indians,
without knowing the real objects of the expedition,
were there to see.   One can easily believe that it
was a great event in the wilderness country.   The
ever-faithful Indian Istikus was there as leader of
the Indians; as they sat mounted upon their ponies,
they added picturesqueness to the group.

The sun was just gilding the treetops along the
Walla Walla as it wended its swift and winding
way like a silver thread in the distance.   The last
adieu had been said, and the Doctor emerged

from his room and mounted his horse. The faithful old dog, which had run by the side of his master in hundreds of journeys along blind trails, was to be permitted to accompany them, barked impatiently.

They were off, an imposing little cavalcade with Whitman and General Lovejoy in the lead, the Indians led by old Istikus following, the pack mules in the rear, while the old dog ran barking up and down the line as if he was responsible commander of the entire outfit.

I have many times in the years since stood upon the ground of this historic scene, and tried to picture it in my mind, in the full grandeur of its intentions and achievements. I have since marched with great armies with music and banners, bright equipments, guns gleaming in the sunlight and their pageantry was imposing, but I most like to catch the spirit of the history they were all making, and it has seemed as if this little band in the wilderness, made up of Christian and savage life was, even in its simplicity, more notably an expression of God's leadings, when I view them in the light of the great events which followed.

Nor can the reader forget to honor the heroic little Christian American woman, who looking through her tear-dimmed eyes, as she waved farewells to her departing husband until the hills away toward the Blue Mountains hid him from view.

After going to her silent and deserted room, she wrote:

"I look from my window and see the grave of our dear child, surely God will take care of my noble husband and return him to me!"

Love is the greatest word in the English language, and when united to Faith, it lifts the heaviest burdens of life. Who can measure the power of the prayers of one faithful, trusting soul, in guiding that heroic little band over the dangers of their unknown way? Possibly some reader may scoff at such sentiment, but unnumbered instances have proved that there comes an emergency in every human life, when the soul, if reason is not clouded, cries out in prayer to a Being higher than itself.

The cavalcade is made up of rapid riders. The favorite gait of Cayuse horses is a lope, and small as they are, carry a heavy man fifty and sixty miles per day. But as the journey was to be a long one, they selected the finest horses to be found, only those thoroughly broken and tested. They knew the value of caring for their animals in the earlier stages, and lessened their speed.

The first four hundred and fifty miles to Fort Hall was made in eleven days. The Indians, except two to look after the animals, had returned to Waiilatpui.

At Fort Hall their old friend, Captain Grant, was still in command, and when he learned of the

proposed journey to the States, openly protested
that "it was madness to attempt it at this season
of the year." Undoubtedly Captain Grant this time
was right, even if Whitman had proved him, to his
chagrin, wrong about the wagon in 1836. "It so
happened" that a company of scouts just then
reached the fort, and confirmed all Captain Grant
had said, and more. They reported that the snow
in many of the cañons was from ten to twenty feet
deep, and badly drifting. The Silent Man listened,
and sat thinking. He knew those mountains and
cañons, and could readily believe the statement of
the scouts, and the old Captain, who was an admirer
of Whitman, felt certain that he would give up his
dangerous expedition and return home. But he
did not yet know his man.

The Old Map

Whitman was face to face with a new problem.
As he prayed and pondered, a new inspiration came
to him. We have no reason to believe that such
an idea had occurred to the missionaries, when discussing the dangers of the journey by the route
they knew. We have no knowledge that even
Whitman had ever before studied the possibilities
of a new and undiscovered way to the States.

The old trappers and scouts sat around the stove
swapping stories of bears, mountain - lions, of
Indians, and wonderful escapes. Whitman, upon

looking up, discovered an old United States map hanging upon the wall. It at once attracted his attention, and he brought it to the light and began to study. It had the outlines of all the great West as far as geographers of that day knew and understood. The ranges of the mountains were nearly accurately pictured. "The great Stony," the Sierra and Coast ranges, the Shasta, and Wind River, and the possible passes were marked, so as to give some idea of the lay of the land.

The thought came to him, why not strike west and south and get between the great ranges so as to avoid the earlier snows of winter? He found marked upon the map Fort Uintah, an old abandoned Spanish fort, which came into possession of the United States in 1818, by the Florida treaty. He then began inquiry among the old mountaineers and found a man who knew the blind trail to Uintah, located in what is now northern Utah. He learned also there was an abandoned trail from that point southward. The old scout was ready to pilot them to Uintah, and was at once engaged. At break of day Whitman and Lovejoy were in their saddles en route, led by the guide, not homeward, but upon a voyage of discovery of the unknown way. The route led south through what is now Idaho, thence through Utah leaving Great Salt Lake to the right. General Lovejoy gives very indistinct notes, not sufficiently clear to accurately verify locations.   He kept a record of daily events, but Whitman never a line.   Lovejoy writes:

"From Fort Hall to Uintah we met with terribly severe weather. The deep snow caused us to lose much time. At Uintah we took a new guide to Fort Uncompagra in old Spanish territory, which place we safely reached. There we hired a new guide, and while passing over a high mountain on the trail toward Grand River, we encountered a terrible snow storm which compelled us to seek shelter in a deep, dark cañon. We made several attempts to pass on, but were driven back, and detained ten days. We finally got well upon the mountain again, when we met with a violent storm of snow and wind, which almost blinded us, maddened the animals, and made them nearly unmanageable. Finally the guide stopped and said, 'I am lost and can lead you no farther' In this dire dilemma, adds General Lovejoy, Dr. Whitman got off his horse, and kneeling in the snow, committed his little company, his loved wife, his work, and his Oregon to the Infinite One for guidance and protection. The lead pack mule being left to himself by the guide pricked up his long ears, turning them this way and that, and began plunging through the snowdrifts, The Mexican guide called out, 'Follow this old mule, he will find the camp if he lives long enough to reach it.' "

And he did lead them to the still burning fire they had left in the morning in the deep, dark cañon.   The instinct of dumb animals is a wonderful gift, superior to that of wise men.   The writer has, twice in his life, been rescued by his horse when hopelessly lost.   One instance I will recite, simply to impress a lesson of kindness upon my young readers for dumb animal life.   Two of us, in a large hunting party in Arkansas, got separated from the rest, and found ourselves in the back-water of the Mississippi River, which was many miles away. My companion was an old woodsman, and pretended to know his direction. He assured me "We will come out all right." He led on and on for hours, the water growing constantly deeper. I finally called to him and pointed to the water-mark on the trees as high as our heads as we sat on our horses. I said to him: "You are lost, now I am going to trust to my horse to lead me from danger." He insisted he knew the way, but followed. My horse was a sleepy old fellow, and I gave him a little cut with a whip to wake him up, then gave him a loose rein to go as he pleased. He wound around fallen trees and brush until he got his direction, then turning nearly at a right angle, struck a line like a surveyor, and in two hours we were upon dry land and in camp.

But to our story. They were safely in camp, by a roaring log fire, the deep cañon protecting them from the raging winds. As they discussed with thankful hearts the perils of the day, from which they had been rescued, they made plans for to-morrow, but here the guide spoke up and said, "I go back, I cannot take you over this mountain." General Lovejoy says, "Whitman talked and plead with the guide until a late hour, but

LOST IN THE ROCKIES.

could not change his mind.   To any except such a
character as Whitman, the situation would have
been indeed hopeless; but before he slept his
plans were made.   He said to General Lovejoy:
"You stay here in the cañon and recuperate the
stock, and I will return to the fort and get a new
guide.   At the first streak of dawn the men were
mounted and on their way.   It was a cheerless
wait for Lovejoy, but he had the companionship of
his dog, and he busied himself in cutting bunch
grass and tender twigs for the animals and bringing
in logs for his fire.   The General says, "Whitman
was gone just one week, when the old dog heard
his distant halloo and answered it with a rejoicing
bark."   He and his new guide, hungry and tired,
were soon enjoying the bright log fire, always the
crowning comfort of camp-life.

I trust that my readers may all live to have a
camp-fire experience.   Permit me to tell you of
one great camp-fire, near the summit of the
Sierras, which lives in the memory after nearly
fifty years of busy life.   Our pack-train had been
toiling up the mountain, hoping for a resting-place,
when our scouts came and reported.   Following
them along winding paths which grizzlies and
Indians had made, around the rugged rocks, we
reached a beautiful little valley covered with luxuri-
ant grass.   We picketed our tired animals in the

meadow, built a great fire of cedar logs against a marble wall straight up for a thousand feet, sang songs, sounded the bugle, and listened to the scores of echoes from the mountain peaks. But we were young and ready to enjoy nature's grand scenes.—Nowhere are they grander than in our own Western mountains.

But our heroic snow-bound travelers were burdened with far too much anxiety to enjoy nature in her magnificent winter adornment. Their eyes were not upon the lofty mountain peaks, but far along unknown trails towards the nation's capital. After they had succeeded in passing the well-nigh impassable mountains, they struck a more level country with sheltered valleys having a bountiful supply of wood and good water. I have often asked myself, when pondering over these events, was it a simple accident that the old scouts reached Fort Hall that October night and turned Whitman and Lovejoy a thousand miles off their direct route? That year the snow lay unusually deep all over the great plains. Had they started and been able to have crossed the Rockies, they would have met snow-covered, treeless plains, and for weeks at a time would have had to go without fires, having to depend upon the *Bois de vache* for fuel, which, covered deep with the snow, would have been impossible to find. This, with the lack of grass for the animals, would have made the route, not only impracticable, but nearly impossible. The scout and the old map seemed insignificant events, but yet how often they and their kind loom up in grand proportions. They may be marked by the thoughtless as mere happenings, but it is not a tax upon reason to believe that the soul attuned to listen and receive ever has a guidance higher than the wisdom of men.

This detention in the cañon and along other parts of the route caused the scant supplies to run lower. The bears were holed up in their winter quarters, they could have found deer and elk, had they stopped and hunted; but Whitman's maxim was forever, "travel, travel." He led upon the trail from morning until night, with eyes ever to the front. General Lovejoy tells us they finally reached a great emergency, and the first animal sacrificed to keep them from starving was the faithful old dog. I doubt not, that some of my young readers will stop to criticize so noble a man as Whitman for having any part in such an act, and the writer would sympathize with the sentiment. The dog is man's closest friend, that clings to him when all others forsake him. Seventy-four years ago, when the author's parents came to the Western wilderness across the Alleghanies, we had a great dog named Watch. He kept guard over us children as we rambled through the woods and along the way, as if he were wholly responsible for our safety. He grew old and nearly helpless. A conference was held among the older members, and it was thought merciful to put him out of his obvious misery, and an old friend of the family was selected for the task. I believe that after all three-quarters of a century of years the children, who loved the old dog, never quite forgave his executioner.

General Lovejoy tells us none of the particulars, but it is reasonable to suppose that Whitman was not consulted at all in the matter, and likely knew nothing of it until long after. The second animal used for food was one of the pack mules. They knew if they could live until they reached Taos, in New Mexico, they could secure supplies, and trade their broken-down stock for fresh animals. So they made forced marches.

I have indulged in only enough description of locality as to keep in touch with the travelers, and to note historic events. To-day the same scenes they viewed are the wonderlands of thousands of tourists each year.

They Reach Grand River

A little incident at Grand River reveals Marcus Whitman's indomitable spirit. It is a deep, dangerous, treacherous river, and many an immigrant has lost his life in the Grand or the Green river. The water is icy cold, even in mid-summer.

When the bold group of travelers stood on the bank they found a stream six hundred feet wide, two hundred feet on each side ice, and two hundred in the middle rolled the rapid torrent. The guide shook his head and said, "It is impossible! We cannot cross." Whitman replied, "We must cross, and now." He got down from his horse, cut a strong cottonwood pole about eight feet long. Mounting his horse, he put the pole upon his shoulder, and said, "Now push us in." The guide and the General skated them to the brink, and "horse and rider," says the General, "entirely disappeared, coming to the surface some distance below." The horse soon found footing and made for the shore, where Whitman broke the ice with his pole, and helped his horse to the firm ice." He soon had a rousing fire from the logs and driftwood. Those conversant with animal habits know that when the lead animal has passed any point, however dangerous, the rest are eager to follow. The General and guide broke the ice for a roadway to the water, and each seizing a tail, were towed safely to the farther shore.

They Reach Santa Fé

Upon reaching Santa Fé, in New Mexico, they felt quite in touch with civilization. They would no longer have to grope in the dark, along doubtful and unknown trails, but it all the more made Whitman anxious to push forward. They paused only long enough to inquire for news from the States, and to purchase a few needed supplies. It was still a long journey, and as it proved, more perilous to life than any portion they had already passed. Their next point was Bent's Fort on the head waters of the Arkansas River, now in Colorado. It was a cheerless, dreary plains journey, with none of the magnificent scenery of the mountain route to keep them company. Water was often scarce, as well as wood, except along the small streams. The intensely cold winter and deep snows had made the big gray wolves a menace to life of men and beasts. One very cold night they reached a little river which had no wood on the side they camped, but was plentiful on the opposite bank. Whitman seized his ax, but found the ice would break under his feet. He then lay flat upon the ice, wormed himself across, skated a bountiful supply across the glossy surface, and then returned in safety as he had gone.

Unfortunately, one of his heavy blows split his ax-handle. When he returned to his tent, he took a piece of rawhide, wrapped the spliced pieces carefully, and threw it down at the door of the tent. In the morning it was discovered that some thieving wolf attracted by the rawhide had stolen the implement, and they never saw it again.   Had this occurred two months before, it would have been regarded as an irreparable disaster.

Four days before reaching Bent's Fort they met Colonel Bent's son with a pack-train en route to El Paso.   He informed them that in two days a company of fifty packers would leave the fort for St. Louis, and that there would not be another until towards spring.

He told them that it would be impossible for them with pack animals to reach the fort before the departure of the company.   Whitman was at once aroused by the information.   He proposed that he should take his blankets and two days' provision, make a forced march, and catch the convoy, while General Lovejoy and the guide could bring on the pack animals and remain at the fort, recuperate the stock, and meet him on the Missouri border in the spring.   This was agreed to, and Whitman started on his lonely ride to Bent's.   General Lovejoy and the guide moved on leisurely, reaching Bent's Fort four days later.   They were astonished and alarmed when told that the Doctor had not arrived.

Whitman is Lost

General Lovejoy stated the whole case to Colonel Bent, who was at once aroused to action. He started runners after the company, ordering them to go into camp on the Cottonwood, and await further commands.

"He sent out his best scouts in the search. Myself, guide, and one of the scouts passed up the banks of the Arkansas for one hundred miles, knowing if Whitman was alive he would make for the river. Every night our camp would be surrounded by hungry, gaunt, gray wolves, which as they were shot down would be torn in pieces and devoured by their fellows."

This gave them great uneasiness about Whitman, alone and without a shelter. They encountered some Indians who told them they had met a white man two days before who was hunting for Bent's Fort, and they had pointed out the way to him. They, in all haste, retraced their steps, along the way the Indians directed, and in an hour after they reached the fort Whitman came in greatly fatigued, and well-nigh despairing. But wearied as he was, he was deeply touched with Colonel Bent's kindness and thoughtfulness, and was buoyed up with new heart and hope that after all the hardships of the long journey he was yet able to prosecute it to the end. In the early morning he was in the saddle upon a fresh horse, with a good guide, and ready to ride forty miles before night to the camp on the Cottonwood, with credentials which would give them safe convoy to St. Louis. General Lovejoy, the guide, and all the stock remained until the next convoy was sent out in the spring, and found Whitman upon the Missouri border.   In that early day the route from Bent's Fort to St. Louis was invested by bands of outlaws, as well as savage wild beasts, so that an escort of well-armed men was a necessity for all travelers.   Thus a good Providence seemed from the outset to have guided the little band through all its perils in safety.

They Reach St. Louis

Dr. Barrows, in his interesting book, "Oregon, the Struggle for Possession," says:

"Upon the arrival of Whitman in St. Louis, it was my good fortune that he should be quartered as a guest under the same roof, and at the same table. Trappers and traders all eagerly asked questions, and he answered all courteously. He in turn asked about Congress; whether the Ashburton treaty had been passed by the Senate; and whether it covered the Northwestern Territory? He then learned, for the first time, that the Ashburton treaty had been signed, even before he left Oregon, and was confirmed by the Senate about the time he was lost and floundering in the snow upon the mountains."

He was eager to learn whether the Oregon question was still pending, and greatly relieved when told that the treaty only covered a little strip of twelve thousand acres, up in Maine, and that Oregon was left untouched in its boundaries. Dr. Barrows continues:

"Marcus Whitman once seen, and in one's family circle, telling of his business, for he apparently had but one, was a man not to be forgotten by the writer. He was of medium height, more compact than spare, a stout shoulder, and a large

head covered with iron-gray hair. He carried himself awk-
wardly. He seemed built as a man for whom more stock had
been furnished than used systematically and gracefully. He
was not quick in motion or speech, and no trace of a fanatic,
but he was a profound enthusiast. He wore coarse, fur garments, with buckskin breeches. He had a buffalo overcoat
with a head hood for emergencies, with fur leggins and foot
moccasins. If my memory is not at fault, his entire dress
when on the street did not show an inch of woven fabric."

We copy thus fully Dr. Barrows's description of
Whitman and his dress, and it agrees with other
descriptions less complete, as we trace him to Cin-
cinnati, and again to the door of his old cherished
friend, Dr. Parker, and have the testimony of his
son, Professor Parker, who opened the door of his
father's home to admit the guest in strange cos-
tume. Whitman had little confidence in his own
power of oratory, and was even timid, while
brave. He knew the persuasive eloquence of his
old associate, and his enthusiasm for Oregon, and
he had hoped and expected to have his help to
plead for Oregon in Washington. But the Doctor
was confined to his room by ill health, and it was
impossible for him to undertake the journey. Glad
again to meet his old friend, and sorrowing that he
was not to have his aid in this critical time, he
resumed his way, and reaching Washington, ended
one of the most memorable trans-continental journeys ever recorded.

CHAPTER IX

———

*Whitman in Washington. His Conference with
President Tyler and Secretary Webster and the
Secretary of War. Visits New York and the
American Board, Boston. His Return to the
Frontier and to Oregon.*

THE exact date of Whitman's arrival at the
national capital can be determined only from
letters, but was probably on March 3,
1843, the day before the close of Congress, when,
as usual, there was hurry and confusion. But it
matters little for our purposes, for we have seen
that the "Oregon boundary question had been up,"
and as usual had been ignored, and only the dis-
puted lines upon a few thousand acres up in Maine
had been adjudicated, while the Oregon boundary
line was left in its old place, "up against the
Rocky Mountains," as Senator Benton expressed
it, "the natural, convenient, and everlasting boundary of the United States!" So Whitman had
only to meet the President and his officials and
individual members to press the claims of Oregon.

Washington in that day was not the beautiful
city now seen, and its manners and customs were

wholly different.   It was before the day of enter-
prising newspaper work.   McCullough and Hal-
stead had not then introduced the modern methods
of "the interview" in daily journals, or we should
not now have to depend upon meager details and
verbal messages to tell of this thrilling episode in
American history.   But it requires no imagination
to believe that this heroic pioneer, dressed in
the garb of the plains, attracted full attention.   No
man better knew the opinions of statesmen regarding Oregon, and we may well believe he felt,
modest man as he was, appalled at the magnitude
of the work before him.   But with such a man we
can believe there was no loitering for preparation.
Fortunately the Secretary of War was an old school
fellow of Whitman's and arranged for a speedy
conference with the President and his Secretary of
State, Webster, the latter the well-known active
enemy of Oregon.   Nothing is more discouraging
to a writer than just such an occasion when giants
meet in combat, and to be unable to report the
words and acts of the actors, except from scrappy
notes and verbal reports.   Whitman never left
any written record of that great discussion, for he
never wrote a note in his life for the purpose of
exalting himself in public estimation.

For the story of the great ride we are wholly
dependent upon General Lovejoy's notes and utter-

ances.   And upon the return journey to Oregon,
and during the long rides, the General says,
"Whitman told me over and over all that was said
and done," in that notable conference at Washington.   Along the same lines we have the testimony
of a score of his associates and co-workers in Oregon, to whom he was in duty bound to make full
report, for they were parties in interest.   So from
such sources we glean our facts, and in their true
spirit and meaning can rest upon them with
much confidence, even if not so satisfactory, as if
written down at the time.

The characters are before us, they had met in
consultation—Marcus Whitman, the man with
frosted hands and feet, dressed in furs and buckskin, who had so loved his country that he had
braved the winter storms, and over unknown ways,
without pay or hoped-for honors or rewards, had
come four thousand five hundred miles to plead for
Oregon to be placed under the flag.   There was
the President, the nation's chief; John Tyler, dignified, clear-eyed, honest, earnest, and as he proved,
sympathetic and anxious to do his whole duty to
the nation; and there was Daniel Webster, known
the nation over as "the Great Orator," and "the
brainy, far-seeing statesman," who was in this case
all out of sympathy with Oregon.   He had re-
peatedly marked its "worthlessness"; he was in

full accord with those who had declared "it would endanger the republic," "was nearer Asia than the United States," and, we may add, that it was fully stated, he was at that very time actively negotiating the trade of Oregon for the Newfoundland fishing banks.

Such, tersely, is a vague pen-picture of three men who met and made history in the executive chamber, noonday, the 5th of March, 1843! The picture is worthy of the skilled brush of some master artist, instead of the poor words of the writer. It matters not if their work failed to be conclusive, it was but forging a link in the golden chain of the nation's grandeur, which had it been severed, no imagination can measure the calamity that would have resulted.

It is the pride of the whole loyal people that the humblest citizen with something important to say may have audience with the nation's chief official. President John Tyler was no exception, and when notified of Whitman's wishes by Secretary of War Porter, he arranged to give him audience without delay. The President was, every day and hour, importuned to meet men, who came to beg for office or honors or emoluments of some kind, but as he learned from Secretary Porter, this man from Oregon was not of that kind he was curiously anxious to meet him. As we have stated,

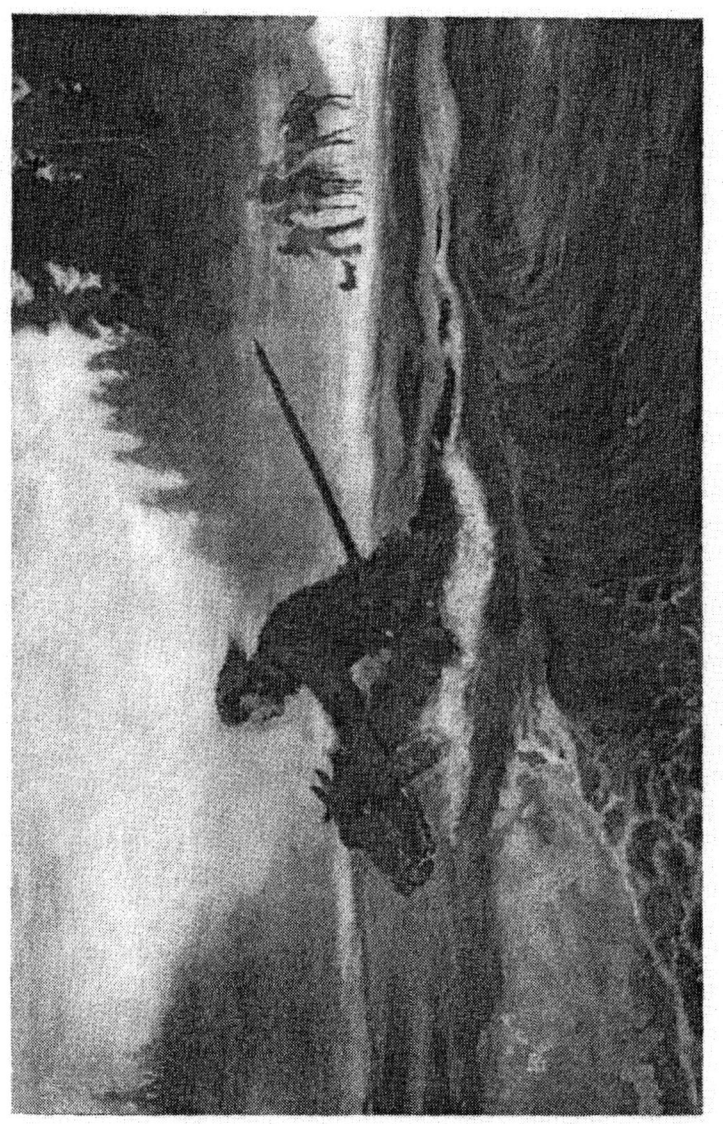

WHITMAN CROSSING GRAND RIVER

we make no effort to report speeches. It is
well known that "the Silent Man" when aroused
was strong and eloquent.   Upon that long journey,
with the weight and importance of his mission
pressing upon him, my readers can well believe
that Whitman's words were strong and true and
impressive.   As he told it to his friends, he dwelt
upon the marvelous fertility of the soil, and the
great crops of grain and fruits his fields and gardens and orchards had produced for six years; how
stock ranged the pastures, fat the year round, without protection or feed from barns.   He told of the
magnificent forests, not equaled in other portions
of the world, of the undoubted mineral riches in
mountains, of the pure water in springs, flowing
rivers navigable for the greatest ships, and of the
inviting, balmy, healthful climate.   Who could
describe better than Whitman the grandeur of the.
Oregon country, destined, as he hoped, "for millions
of American people!"   It was then that the keen
Webster made the remark, but "Doctor, how can you
ever make a wagon-road for American immigration
to Oregon?" and received the prompt reply, "There,
Mr. Secretary, you have been deceived and mis-
informed.   There is a wagon-road to Oregon now,
and I made it and took a wagon over it six years
ago, and it is there to-day!"   That is the triumph
of the old wagon turned into a cart with its front

wheels lashed to its sides.　The patient, good little wife, in the years before, was sorrowing over the labors of her husband in his hard work, and mourned through many pages of her diary, as we have seen, over the folly of hauling along "the old wagon."　She was not permitted to look into the future and hear how the Indian boys' "Old Click-Click - Clackety - Clackety" would strike dumb the nation's greatest orator.　Nor is it at all likely that Whitman himself ever dreamed of such results.　He simply obeyed a silent voice within, as was his rule of life, and old "Click," amid trials and perils never half told, rolled on, and made history.

Whitman referred also to the current rumors, of the purpose of "trading Oregon for the Newfoundland fishing banks," and said, "Mr. President, you had far better trade all New England than Oregon for the fishing banks!"　This was a hard blow at the great secretary, who was as much wrapped up in New England as New England was in him.　He referred to the treaty of 1818–1828, and "its understood meaning in Oregon, that whichever of the two nations settled Oregon should own and hold it"; he said, all I ask is, that you make no barter of Oregon until we can settle loyal Americans there in numbers sufficient to hold that which is their own.　I hope to help lead such a band this

summer, a group already gathering upon the Missouri, worthy of your consideration and protection.
I do not here pretend to give the exact words of
Whitman, for reasons stated, but they are truthful
to the spirit, as verified by scores of men, to whom
all the scenes were related, and whose veracity
cannot be doubted.   Dr. Spalding says:

"Whitman concluded his address by saying, 'Mr. President,
all that remains for me to say is, to ask, that you will not barter
any of Oregon or allow English interference, until I can lead a
band of stalwart American settlers across the plains, which I
hope and expect to do.'   To this President Tyler, deeply
impressed, promptly and positively replied, 'Dr. Whitman,
your long ride and frosted limbs speak of your courage and
patriotism, and your missionary credentials are good vouchers
for your character,' and he unhesitatingly granted his simple
requests."

Whitman then held a long conference with the
Secretary of War, and agreed that he at an early a
date as possible would prepare an act which could
be laid before Congress, covering the important
points in the territorial organization of Oregon, and
also a second article upon the strategic points
along the immigrant route, where forts, resting places and protection could be vouchsafed.
Both these important documents were written by
Whitman during the summer, and are to be found
in the archives of the war department in Washington, and can be read in the Appendix to my larger
work, "How Marcus Whitman Saved Oregon."

He held conference with many members of Congress, and felt that his work at the national capital was ended.

Whitman was not a man to loiter, and we next hear of him closeted with the staunch friend of Oregon, Horace Greeley of the New York Tribune. Greeley knew and admired a heroic character, and he highly complimented Whitman and his work in the Tribune. He proceeded to Boston to report to the American Board, to receive any reprimand for violation of rules and to transact minor affairs of the missions in Oregon. The enemies of Whitman have again and again gone over the old records of the American Board to find some severe rebuke to the man who "dabbled in politics." But if any rebuke was offered, it was careful to make no record of it. But it may be said the governors of the American Board evidently failed to comprehend in their anxiety to keep clear of all complications between "Church and State," that they were dealing with an *inspired man*, who had rendered the greatest possible service to the nation and to Protestant Christianity. They did another good act, either through pride for one of their missionaries or from generosity they sent him to a tailor shop for a complete suit of cloth clothes, which his own slim pocket-book could not afford. It took the American Board just fifty years from the date

of his death to see that the man in furs and
leather breeches from Oregon, who stood humbly
before them upon that occasion, was one of the
grandest characters, as Christian and patriot,
that they ever before or since enrolled as missionary! They waked up to that fact in 1897,
when the great organization assembled in annual
council, called attention to the fact, that it was
"the fiftieth anniversary of the death of Dr. Marcus
Whitman, an eminent missionary of the Board,"
and appointed special services to be held in several
leading cities, and a general observance of that day.
It was a thoughtful, educational, Christian act,
which, if the old martyr could from his eternal
mansion look down and hear, would make him
glad.

The good Presbyterians who were a part of the
American Board at that time, and were not then
at all anxious to share in any honors to Whitman, latterly saw new light in something of the
character grandeur of the neglected missionary.
They caused a beautiful statue of Dr. Marcus Whitman to be placed in their Witherspoon building
at Philadelphia. To the boys and young men, let
me say the lesson in this is, that all good things
come to the good who wait! Stand true for the
right. It was that which has resurrected the
name and honor of Whitman, after long years of

neglect, and will make his name shine, and glow with increasing luster, as the years come and go!

As Mrs. Whitman playfully wrote her father and mother, "I expect my dear husband will be so full of his great mission that he will not take time to tell you of home affairs, I will do so." That was in a measure true. He made a hurried visit to his mother in her home, to his wife's parents, and to his brother, who had moved West. But his eyes and thoughts and hopes were ever westward. He had heard from General Lovejoy, who was on the ground, of the bright prospect of a large company for Oregon. As the spring months opened in 1843, there were stirring times along the border, such as never before seen. Great wagons, with white canvas covers, drawn by long-horned oxen, sturdy mules, and horses, herds of fine cattle to stock the new farms, with from eight hundred to a thousand men, women, and children, with their household treasures, were there. They had received the same inspiration as their fathers who had peopled the great West across the Alleghanies, and the motto still was, "Westward the Star of Empire takes its way." Such were the inspiring conditions which greeted Whitman when he reached the border. He was a man of great faith, and firmly believed in success, but such an imposing body filled his soul with gratitude and thankfulness.

The company was made up mainly from the rural districts, strong, muscular men, their wives and children, and eager young people. There were many anxious mothers, who saw the responsibility of the great undertaking, and whose perils women intuitively feel more certainly than men. Who can tell the secret of that sudden gathering of pioneer heroes, on the banks of "the Great Muddy" in 1843? True, the old missionaries had written many letters. New immigrants had done the same. But Congress and the national authorities had done nothing but ridicule, and in no single case had lent a helping hand. There must have been some secret telepathetic power which had sounded a call!

True, Whitman and Lovejoy had been busy, but neither one ever made claim of inducing the great immigration of 1843. The honor was sufficient for them, as the only men acquainted with the road, to lead the great company to the promised land in safety. But the enemies of these missionaries, especially of Whitman, tried so often to make light of his eminent services, that the Rev. Dr. Myron Eells of Twana, Washington, some years ago, sat down and wrote to every living pioneer of that immigration he could locate (and he knew most of them), and asked the question, "Did Dr. Whitman induce you to immigrate to Oregon in 1843?" Two-fifths replied, "Yes."

The last weeks of April and the first of May found most of the immigrants pulled out upon the road, in companies of fifties and hundreds. They were in the Indian country on the first day of travel, and not sure how such an invasion would be received by the savages, they were warned to keep compact, and in bodies large enough for protection. The Indians, men, women, and children, swarmed about every camp, and watched every movement. They were invariably treated kindly, and responded with kindness. The warriors sat upon their horses stolidly by the trails and watched the long wagon-trains, the herds of cattle, and especially the women and children, the like of which had never before invaded their domain. The weeks of travel across the grass-grown, flower-covered prairies of Kansas and Nebraska was a picnic occasion for the immigrants. It was well that it was so. They did not have many afterward.

The wagons were soon strung out over a long line. Dr. Whitman did not start with the head of the company. In a letter to a friend he wrote, "I remained behind until the last wagon was on the road." There were many who needed advice as to proper outfit, what to take, and what to leave, many who needed encouragement to start at all. When all had moved he rode rapidly to the

MARMADUKE ISLAND.   (B. H. Gifford, photo.)

head of the column, to overtake it before it reached the Platte, the first wide river to be crossed.

The Platte is not a dangerous river if forded properly, but it looks threatening to timid people. It is nearly one mile wide, and it is about breast deep in ordinary stages. It runs over a bed of sand, and the secret of safety is to keep on the sand bars and keep moving. A halt, even for a few minutes, allows the feet of animals, or the wagon wheels to sink into the sands, and they are not easily extricated. Upon reaching the bank of the river, horsemen upon the best horses survey the route by zigzagging up and down, finding the shallowest water upon the bars, which are constantly shifting. The train of wagons are arranged to follow each other, a dozen or more yards apart, with horsemen at each vehicle to give immediate assistance in case of break or accident. The first driver keeps his eye upon the careful guides, picking the shallowest route. Careless endeavors to pull straight across, instead of pulling two miles around to gain one, involved trouble. The murky water is surcharged with sand, which is forever blown into it as it winds through the great plains, and is the source of the Missouri River's excessive supply of sand. It proves to be pure water if allowed to stand and settle. A bucket of water standing over night in the morning will be clear, with an inch of pure sand on the bottom. If the old maxim is true, "A fellow needs sand in his craw," he easily gets it on the Platte. Our immigrant party, wisely directed, forded the river safely with all its stock. Care was taken in fording all rivers to place heavy articles not easily injured by water low in the bed of the wagon.

The Buffalo Country

Here the caravan entered the buffalo country, where they were likely to meet large bodies of armed Indians who came there from long distances, to lay in their winter stores of meat and furs and skins. Many of these tribes were jealous of each other, and of white men who intruded upon their domain on such occasions, and bloody encounters frequently occurred while upon the way. The caravan had elected a captain to direct affairs and a guide to make orders for travel. But now they found so many questions arising in this large company, that a council or superior court was organized, from which there was no appeal. It held its sessions at night and upon rest days, and many of the members of that court upon the plains, after in the territory and states of Oregon, Washington, and Idaho, held the highest offices of trust and honor.

A halt to lay in a supply of buffalo meat was looked forward to with great satisfaction. But it was found impracticable for so large a company to make a permanent halt, so they kept moving.

The hunters in large numbers went out each morning, with pack horses, and came in loaded at night with spoils of the chase. The noble bison was there by the million.

When reaching the dusty alkaline plains, where both good water and grass were scarce, naturally the best tempered people often turned grumblers. One of the chief causes of complaint laid before the superior court was that which arose between the horse companies and the cattle companies. They did not agree well together. The court decided to divide the caravan into two columns, "the horse" and "the cow" column. In 1876 the Honorable Jesse Applegate, a member of that immigration, delivered an address before The Historical Society of Oregon, entitled "A Day with the Cow Column." It is one of the most precise and graphic pictures ever drawn of life as it was, in this advance column of civilization, destined for its great work in the future Pacific states. The last third of the distance of that memorable journey proves the courage of the American, and at the same time arouses our commiseration and pity. I passed over the larger portion of the same road a few years later, with goggles drawn over my eyes, and a handkerchief bound about my face, as a defense from the dust and the myriad buffalo gnats, and can the more easily sympathize with those hundred mothers, often forced to travel on foot with little and well-nigh helpless children pulling at their skirts. As I think, I can but say, "O the pity of it!"

Mr. Applegate remarks:

"There was no time to pause and recruit the hungry stock, or to hunt for the withered herbage, for a marauding enemy hung upon the rear, and hovered on our flanks, and skulked in ambuscade in front. The road was strewn with dead cattle, abandoned wagons, and every article of household goods, even the sacred keepsakes. The failing strength of teams, required shorter couplings so as to save a few pounds. An ox or a horse would fall. Men would remove the yoke or harness, and secure a substitute from the almost equally tired animals in the corral."

Oh, it is well for the sons and daughters of these states of the Pacific, as well as the tourist in his parlor car, as they look upon flower-decked meadows, waving wheat-fields, orchards, and homes of comfort, with beauty everywhere, to remember the heroic deeds of heroic men and women who won for them this grand inheritance.

When the immigrants reached Fort Hall they met Captain Grant, who made the old appeal: "Leave your wagons, impossible to take them, no wagon-road to Oregon." He showed them the many wagons already left as proof of his statement. But here comes Whitman, who says, "Men, you have with incredible hardship brought your wagons

thus far, they are a necessity for your wives' and
children's comfort, even their lives.   They will be
invaluable to you when the end of the journey is
reached.   I took a wagon, made into a eart, to
Fort Boise six years ago."   And thus "Old
Click," on its last round, gave out its best blessing, which it conferred upon tired mothers and
little children.   The company took Whitman's advice, and the wagons rolled on.   His watch-word
was, "Travel, travel, travel, nothing else will bring
rest and the end of the journey."

Upon reaching Snake River, the doctor devised
an ingenious and safe method for the weaker teams
to cross.   There were still remaining about one
hundred wagons, which Whitman arranged in one
long line, placing the strong teams in front.   The
wagons rear and front were then roped together
and the procession started with fifty men on
horseback, pulling upon a long rope in front, while
others attended the variotis teams to keep every
one in line and moving.

It was a daring venture, but so well managed
that the deep and dangerous river, the worst upon
the route, was passed without accident.   Many
years ago the author, while making a talk in the
opera house at Walla Walla, where many of the
old pioneers and their descendants were gathered,
recited the incident of the crossing of the Snake.

After the close of the meeting a venerable old gentleman came to me and taking my hand said:

"Yes, that story of the crossing of the Snake is true, I was there. But I had four yoke of as good steers as ever pulled in yokes, and I was determined they should not be tied up in that long string of wagons to drown. I stood upon the bank and waited until the whole line was fully one-third across when I whipped in. I got about a quarter of a mile from shore, when I struck deep water, and felt my wagon floating, and soon oxen and wagon were facing squarely up stream, and the oxen barely getting foothold. I saw it only a question of time when we would drift into the deep water below and be lost. Just then I heard a shout, 'hold them steady,' 'hold them steady,' and I looked and saw a man rushing through the water, and as he came in reach he deftly dropped a rope over the horns of the lead ox, and beginning to pull gently said, 'Now whip up.' The noble animals responded, and taking a wide circuit, the water grew shallower, and we reached the shore in safety! And that man was Marcus Whitman!"

At the Snake the doctor met his faithful old Indian Istikus, and a pack-train loaded with flour sent to them by Dr. Spalding. Never was a generous gift so fraught with blessing. He also received letters telling him of the dangerous illness of Mrs. Spalding and urging him to leave all and ride with speed to the Spalding Mission. So the rest of the journey was made under the guidance of Istikus, who knew every foot of the way, and could give excellent advice.

The doctor, mounted upon a fresh horse sent by Dr. Spalding, was soon galloping on his way, and his wonderful ride ended when he reached home a few days later. Less than three weeks after that one hundred wagons, with their precious loads of wearied humanity, rolled down the sides of the Blue Mountains into the grassy, flower-decked meadows of the Walla Walla Valley, and American history made one of its grandest records. Old Glory went up, never to be hauled down while patriots live! The entire land between the oceans was ours. While perhaps one distinctive personage stands conspicuously in the front, there were honors enough to crown the whole band of heroes and heroines which, in 1843, at a critical period, marked plainly the great highway across the continent.

CHAPTER X

Whitman Joins the Great Immigrating Column. The News of the Safe Arrival in Oregon, and its Effects Upon the People. The Part Taken by Dr. Whitman, and Oregon's Importance to the Nation. The Great Political Contest. The Massacre.

THE great immigration of 1843 to Oregon had called out wide attention from the thinking people all over the land. Congressmen in Washington began to hear from the people; still, in both houses of Congress were heard mutterings of "the desert waste" and "dangers of expansion." Lawmakers have a way of listening to the voices of men who make lawmakers, and they heard it on the Oregon question. President Tyler was true to his pledge to Whitman, and if there ever was a thought on the part of Webster to barter off Oregon, it was never heard of again. A great political party saw in it a popular national issue, and emblazoned upon their banners "Oregon and 54' 40° or fight!"

Nobody ever before or since saw such a political upheaval and somersault. The issue elected

both a President and a Congress.   President Tyler
was unwilling to let all the glory of it go to his
political enemies, and in his closing message, gave
large place to the importance of Oregon!   The
incoming President James K. Polk gave about
one-fourth of his entire message to the Oregon
question.

Such was the status of the question within a
year and a half after Whitman's great ride.

The question was up to England, and the western boundary of the United States, which had been
so easily settled in 1842, by compromising on a
few farms in Maine, had to move westward from
its fixed place in "the great Stony Mountains," or
war was imminent.

England, as well as America, was aroused, and
she sent over her experienced minister plenipo-
tentiary Packingham.   James Buchanan represented the United States, and they began their
great task without delay.   We no longer heard the
old congressional cry of "No value in Oregon."
Both nations saw great issues at stake, and keen
and prolonged negotiations resulted.   It was a
battle royal between experienced diplomatists.
Now, please note a prominent fact, this demand to
settle the national dispute began in 1844, and it
was not until April, 1846, that the treaty was
signed, after most laborious efforts.

I wish to impress upon my readers the importance of dates in this, for they emphasize and make clear the timely acts of Whitman. In less than seven months the United States declared war against Mexico, and California was at stake. Suppose England could have foreseen that event, and the nine hundred million dollars of pure gold mined in California and Oregon, during the following ten years, would she have signed the treaty even in 1846? When did that great nation ever allow such a golden opportunity to pass without reserving tribute? Had England been given more time and more thorough knowledge, there is scarcely a doubt but that she would have tenaciously held to Oregon. It would have been easy for her to have joined hands with Mexico, and if so, had the United States held any of her present Pacific possessions, it would have been after a long and desolating war, in which the United States would have been at a great disadvantage, from its small navy at that time.

"I Must Go Now"

You will recollect when Dr. Whitman's old friends at the mission conference recited to him the dangers of such a trip, and said "Wait until spring," he simply and solemnly replied "*I must go now.*" The plain facts of history are the keys that explain that answer! It would not have done "to wait until spring." In all the sacred record, dealing with men's duties, the command is "go," "do," not to-morrow, not next year, but "now." Whitman made no boast to his fellow-missionaries of any ·inspiration, but they were of the class of men who could understand and appreciate his acts. In the glow of light from history, every thoughtful Christian can read their deeper meaning.

No, it would have been all too late had he waited to pilot that great immigration of 1843. No reader can but know, upon the safety of that band of immigrants, the fate of Oregon was dependent for years to come. Had another great Donnelley disaster come to them, and they had·perished, who knows when another would have followed? No, it would not do to "wait until spring." It even then, with an awakened people, required two years to get England's consent to sign the treaty. Then, having Oregon we wanted and needed California. More reason still, great perils were in front, and less than a dozen years later, the existence of the Union was in danger. With the gold of California and Oregon, and the three great loyal states behind the flag, it is easy to see the timeliness of the act, and the immensity of the danger from delay, *not only to Oregon, but to the nation.*

Some' may say, "this is only a supposable case,"

and it would be true, but the facts are that England, through her Hudson Bay Company, had virtually owned and controlled Oregon for nearly half a century, from 1818 up to the day Whitman started upon his great ride, altogether with the official sanction of the American people. There can scarcely be a doubt in regard to it, for reasons before stated, that England expected to continue to hold it all, or at least a large portion of it. Those who shout no danger are blind to historic facts.

Had England at the date mentioned owned Oregon, or any part of it, it is reasonably certain she would have thrown her great influence with the South in that terrible struggle in 1861–1865, when "cotton was king," and when it required all the eloquence of America's greatest orators, backed up by many of England's wisest statesmen, to prevent England at the most critical period of the struggle, "acknowledging the belligerent rights of the South."

Old Glory floats to-day from ocean to ocean, and from lakes to the Gulf the men once at war are at peace: "the gray" and "the blue" have since marched and fought under the same flag, and have rejoiced together alike in its achievements.

The brave pioneers of Oregon, without waiting

THE ASSASSINATION OF DR. WHITMAN.

for authority of Congress, raised the American flag, organized a territorial government, elected officials to make and execute laws, and from 1843 to 1848, without the aid of Congress, by a single official act, they carried on the government as becomes good citizens of the Republic. True, there were murmurings in Congress as of old, but they were only half-hearted, and half in earnest. The final signing of the treaty in 1846 was the doom, however, of the regime of England in Oregon.

England in its Saddle

She did not wait for signatures to the treaty to set on foot an inquiry, as to the loss of Oregon, or who was responsible for it, and how this great immigration from the states had originated. The English company forthwith sent a commission, made up of Messrs. Peel, Park, and Wavaseur, to Oregon, to learn all the facts. When they reached there they had an easy task, for both Englishmen and Americans understood the matter.

When Whitman and Spalding, with their wives, caught up with the convoy of fur-traders, in that memorable journey in 1836, one of the old voyageurs who had felt the iron hand of the Hudson Bay Company, sententiously remarked, as he pointed his finger at the two American women, "There is something the royal Hudson Bay Com-

pany and its masters can't drive out of Oregon!''
And it proved true prophecy. We have already
noted the courtesy and kindness with which Dr.
John McLoughlin, the chief factor, received the
missionaries. The London officials soon learned
that they had to deal with but one man, and he was
in their power.

If that interview between the doctor and these
eminent Englishmen, who had grown great and rich
through his management, could be fully reported,
it would doubtless make interesting reading. However modern historians may differ as to the cause
of the sudden large immigration of Americans to
Oregon, the commissioners from London had no
doubt upon the subject. They made the direct
charge that it was due to McLoughlin's over-kind-
ness to the missionaries, that had he treated them
as he did the American traders, such conditions
would not have existed. It mattered not that the
good old doctor knew that the charge was sub-
stantially true, and yet he arose in righteous indig-
nation, and replied:

"What would you have? Would you have me turn a cold
shoulder on the men of God, who came to do for the Indians,
that which this company had ever neglected to do? If we had
not helped them, and the immigrants of '42 and '43, Fort Vancouver would have been destroyed, and the world would have
treated our inhuman conduct as it deserved. Every officer
of the Company, from governor down, would have been covered with obloquy and the business ruined.''

This conference was about one year and eight months before the signing of the treaty, and the English people and the Hudson Bay Company, while worried over the situation, still had small fear of losing the entire country. They felt sure of at least owning, upon final settlement, all north of the Columbia River. They still expected to undo the work of the man who had for more than a quarter of a century been coining them fortunes, and they promptly turned him adrift, and appointed his successor.

After the treaty was signed, in 1846, and came fully into American possession, the great monopoly continued to show its modesty, and sent in a bill of damages to the United States for $4,950,036.17, of which amount the United States paid in cash $650,000. Then the Company "squatted" upon one of our islands some six miles from shore, raised the English flag, and the United States had another siege lasting thirty years, with threatened war, before the question, "who owns San Juan Island?" was left to the arbitration of the emperor of Germany, who, in 1875, decided in favor of the United States. With this brief history we dismiss the Hudson Bay Company from our further concern, except to note its humane act, in the prompt rescuing of the captive women and children, after the massacre. Still there

is another good thing that should be said of the
Hudson Bay Company.   Under the rule of Dr.
McLoughlin "the great white head chief," the
Indians over so large a district were never before
so well and wisely ruled.   They obeyed his orders
as promptly as loyal subjects to their king.   The
desire in these pages has been to do no injustice,
or make unfair criticism.   There are "trusts" and
"monopolies" in the United States to-day even
more selfish than the Hudson Bay Company.   The
English people were not usurpers in Oregon.
They only accepted and used for the first half of
the nineteenth century, with the full official consent
of the American people, one of our great possessions, which we had marked as "worthless."   It is
well to bear such facts in mind, and thus allow the
mischief done, as well as the good attained, to rest
where it belongs.

Whitman on the March and at the Mission

"Who led the great immigration of 1843 safely
to Oregon?" has often been a subject of discussion.

Upon the safety of that band was that of Oregon
dependent.   Whitman was not the captain of the
caravan, but he was the one man in the cavalcade
who had been three times over the route.   In that
day there was not a guide-book in existence, and
he, with General Lovejoy (who had been over this

route once, and that from Fort Hall twice), was relied upon by captain, guide, and people for advice and direction. It is easy to see the important place he held.

Perhaps no man among the pioneers of Oregon was better qualified to tell of Whitman's services than was the Honorable Jesse Applegate, who was a member of the expedition, and for many years after, one of the most honored citizens of Oregon.

In a great oration, delivered before the State Historical Society of Oregon, in 1876, he calls Dr. Whitman the "good angel of the immigration." In closing his address, after noting many eminent men and their good work, he said:

"Now, I will intrude no other name of that noble band but that devoted man, Dr. Marcus Whitman. His stay with us was transient, but the good he did was permanent. From the day he joined us on the Platte, his indomitable energy was of priceless value to the migrating column, and it is no disparagement to any individual to say, that to no other man are the immigrants of 1843 so deeply indebted for a successful conclusion of their journey as to Dr. Whitman."

Dr. Spalding, who was present at the Whitman Mission when the immigrants reached there, says:

"Hundreds of the immigrants stopped at Waiilatpui to take Whitman by the hand, and many with tears in their eyes, acknowledged their obligations for his untiring labor and skill, which brought them in safety over the weary way."

Whitman was not a politician in the sense the

term is generally used, but only a few months before his death he rode on horseback to Oregon City to induce his old friend Judge Thornton to visit Washington and try to persuade the authorities to organize a territorial government in Oregon. The Judge accepted, and was on that mission at the time of the massacre at Waiilatpui (November 29, 1847).

The Massacre

Whitman was a tireless worker. Frequently. after toiling all day in his fields or upon his buildings, he spent long hours of the night on the rounds to visit his sick; yet he did not fail to see the bad influences used upon the Cayuse Indians.

They feared him and his influence. There had been mutterings of discontent among the Cayuse Indians; too many whites were coming in. There was much sickness among the Indians; the measles had prevailed; with their unsanitary living and barbarous treatment of the sick many had died. They laid it all to the white settlers, and blamed those who encouraged and helped them. Good old Istikus, their faithful Indian friend of many years, had warned them that some of his people had bad hearts toward them, and begged them to go away until their hearts were good again. But how could they go. On the fatal morning when the conspiracy was brought to execution, seventy people were in the mission station, mostly women, children, and sick men worn out by long travel and exposure. It was two hundred and fifty miles to Fort Vancouver by trail or in open boats down the Columbia River. That was the only place of safety, and they could not leave all these people, nor could they take them. Moreover, Whitman still had faith in his Indians, which was partly justified by the facts, as it was proved that no Cayuse could quite bring himself to strike the first blow. But they found one more treacherous who was ready to take the Judas part in the tragedy. He was called Joe Tahamas, a half-breed Canadian, who had come to the mission station several months before hungry, sick, and half-clad. As their custom was they took him in, clothed, fed, and nursed him back to health again. After a time they found him fomenting quarrels among their people, and stirring up their evil passions in various ways. They finally procured him a place as teamster to go to the Willamette River, and hoped their troubles with him were ended. He had returned, and from after evidence, had no doubt been going through the tribe, and with a lying tongue rousing the Indians to a mad passion against their friends and benefactors. Some distant chief of the tribe had armed him with what was known as "The

Charmed Tomahawk." It had long before been presented to them by the warring Sioux, in some great peace talk, and was to bring them victory and good fortune wherever it was used. After the massacre at Waiilatpui and the war following, with the banishment and partial destruction of their tribe, "The Charmed Tomahawk" became "Bad Medicine." No one wished to keep it, but with the old superstition of a living spirit in everything, they feared to destroy it, lest some greater punishment should fall upon them, and it passed from one to another as they would receive it.

The Charmed Tomahawk

An Indian agent, named Logan, learned the story and purchased it, as we may believe, for but a small sum. During the Civil War, in an auction sale for the benefit of The Sanitary Commission, the hatchet with its story was sold for a hundred dollars, and was presented to the legislature of Oregon. It has finally lodged among the treasured relics of the Oregon Pioneer Association in Portland, where it will doubtless be seen by many during the coming summer. The 29th of November, 1847, the fatal morning dawned that ended the career of the devoted missionary band gathered on the Walla Walla. The Doctor no doubt with a heavy heart, after all his warnings, went out on his round of duty, to look after the farm and stock, to visit the sick, and supply any wants of the emigrants camped about them. Returning to the house, he sat down in his office before his desk and was reading with John Sager, one of his adopted boys seated by his side. An Indian came in, saying he was sick and wanted some medicine. While his attention was engaged by him, Tahamas stole silently in, armed with "The Charmed Tomahawk," and with one blow on the back of the head, crushed in the skull, and the poor Doctor sank unconscious to the floor, though he lived for several hours after. The brave boy by his side, drew a small pistol from his pocket, and attempted to shoot the murderer, but was struck down with the same weapon and immediately killed. The Indians then left the house, where there were only women and children, to join the great company gathering outside and find the unarmed men scattered about the place. Two of these badly wounded made their way back to the house, and barred doors and windows as best they could to protect the helpless ones inside. Only four men made their escape unharmed to carry the news to Fort Vancouver and ask for help. Mr. Spalding, one of their fellow missionaries, was on his way, and near Waiilatpui, when the massacre occurred. His little daughter was in Mrs. Whitman's school, a witness of the

whole bloody tragedy, and afterward one of the
captives, carried away by the Indians. From her
descriptions, and that of others who lived to tell
the tale, he wrote a full description of the tragic
scenes to the parents of Mrs. Whitman. It is
needless to say they were too terrible to repeat
in detail. Still it is well to know how the heroic
wife met death, still giving her thought and life
for others. She and one of the young women
had carried the body of her dying husband to
a private room, and she was kneeling by his
side, when the host of savages returned to the
house. Maddened like wild beasts with the
sight of blood, they tore the weak bars from doors
and windows, and with savage war-whoops entered
the house. Their superstitions prevented them
from entering the death chamber, but they began
looting the house and threatening to kill the women
and children, whose frantic cries added terror to
the scene. It was then the heroic wife left the
side of her dying husband, and her safe retreat,
going from one to another trying to comfort and
soothe them. As she walked past a window, a
bullet struck her in the breast; she grasped the
window-sill to keep from falling, and recognized
her murderer as Tahamas, for whom she had done
so much. She exclaimed, "Oh, Joe, is it you!"
It was like the dying cry of Cæsar, when he saw

his old-time friend in the mob about him, "Thou, too, Brutus!" and a sharper pang than her wound gave entered that tender heart. She was carried back to her room. A few hours later the Indians sent word to her that if she would come out they would not harm her, but would go away after they had seen her. She was then too weak from loss of blood to walk, but she asked Mr. Rogers, one of their helpers, and Miss Beulah, a friend, to carry her into the next room, where the Indians had gathered. They had hardly entered it when a volley of shots were fired, and both she and Rogers were pierced by many balls.

Some one now in authority gave an order not to shoot the women and children. The little ones were all gathered in one corner, witnessing the whole terrible scene, but one Indian more humane picked up some blankets and screened it all from their view. One of the men, a guest at the mission, raised a board in the floor and hid himself, wife, and three children beneath. They suffered agony in their imprisonment, with the blood of the murdered ones trickling through the floor upon them. On a visit to Walla Walla and out to the old mission farm, two years ago, we met a very intelligent and interesting lady, who, in the course of conversation, told us that she was one of the three children hidden under the floor during that terrible day and that she was then but a little child the remembrance had never left her, nor could she see an Indian without a shudder. The Indians went at their work leisurely, and seemed anxious to prolong the torture. They knew it was two hundred and fifty miles to Vancouver, and they had no fear of molestation from any other source. For five days they kept up their orgies, guarding against escape of their victims. At the end of that time they began to be anxious for their own safety, and gathering the women and children, forty in number, they started for a friendly tribe to wait for developments.

Runners were sent in haste to Fort Vancouver telling of the disaster, and Chief Factor Ogden of the Hudson Bay Company lost no time in starting for the scene with twenty picked men, boats and provisions. Upon reaching Waiilatpui they found everything in ruins, the houses wrecked, the mill burned, and the dead bodies of eleven men, one boy, besides the bodies of Dr. and Mrs. Whitman. These were all tenderly gathered and buried together, in what has been called ever since "the Great Grave." In the mean time Chief Ogden had sent runners after the Indians, with a peremptory order to return all the captive women and children to him at once, to Fort Walla Walla. For many years the Indians had been accustomed

D. K. PEARSONS, M. D., LL. D

to obey orders from this source, and they thought
it wise now to comply; besides they soon began to
find the helpless captives a burden to feed.
Chief Ogden assured them he would pay them a
handsome ransom if all were brought in safely.
One or two of the chiefs, who were enamored of
the young women, insisted they should be allowed
to keep them in captivity and make them their
wives. It required strategy, threats, and promise of larger reward before that trouble was overcome. All were finally brought in, except three
delicate children, one the adopted child of the
doctor, and two others, who perished from exposure. Ogden gave the Indians blankets, powder,
lead, and other articles they demanded, to the value
of five hundred dollars, and all were conveyed to
Fort Vancouver, and places of safety.

Four men only escaped the massacre. One of
these was Dr. Spalding. He was on his way to
visit the doctor on business, and to see his little
daughter, who was a pupil in Mrs. Whitman's
school. When nearing the station he met one of
the Jesuit priests, who told him of the disaster.
He immediately retraced his steps, fully expecting a like work at his own mission. He reached
home the second night in a dazed condition. His
Nez Perces, when they heard of it, rallied around
him some five hundred of their bravest warriors,

and escorted Dr. and Mrs. Spalding quickly to a
place of safety.   Their little daughter Eliza, nearly
ten, was rescued and returned to them.

Cayuse Thought the Flurry Over

The Cayuse received their presents and seemed
to think their work was over.   In this they were
mistaken.   The hardy old pioneers of Oregon, who
loved and honored Dr. and Mrs. Whitman, arose
as one man, and in winter, without tents or proper
equipments, moved down upon the Cayuse country.
I do not intend to burthen my readers with the
story of a long, desolating Indian war.   It was a
bloody and savage contest, where General Phil H.
Sheridan was initiated into active military life and
won his first honors.

The leaders in the massacre, Tilcokait, Tahamas,
Ouichmarsum, Klvakamus, and Sichsalucus were
arrested and hung at Oregon City, just before the
author reached there.   In 1850 one of the most mis-
erable of the villains, Tarntsaky, was killed while being arrested.   My room-mate in Oregon in 1850, the
late Samuel Campbell of Idaho, spent the winter
and spring of 1847 at the Whitman Mission, and
never tired in telling of the lovely Christian character of Mrs. Whitman, of her kindness and patience
to whites and Indians alike.   She had retained
the same glorious musical voice, and life wherever
she went was filled with what Matthew Arnold

would call "sweetness and light." Mr. Campbell
said while he was a prisoner at Grand Ronde, old
Tarntsaky one day boasted in his presence that he
took the scalp from Mrs. Whitman's head, and told
him of the long, golden, silky hair. He said,
"Prisoner as I was, it was all I could do to keep
my fingers from his throat." The many tribes
around sided with the Cayuse, except the Nez
Perces, and the whole land was closed to white
settlers for over ten years, as the state government deemed it impossible to protect the scattered
settlements.

The Result

The final result was that the tribes engaging in
the war were all removed to distant reservations, and
forty thousand square miles of rich territory were
opened to settlement. Thus the great sacrifice resulted for the good of the people. The work of
the American Board in sending missionaries to
Oregon has sometimes been called "a disaster"
and "failure." Was it? What could have been
grander work for any Christian man than Whitman's
brave part in saving the whole great territory to the
Union? Patriotism is a part of Christianity, and
an important part. That man is a feeble Christian
who does not love his home and fatherland.

The American Board never claimed, or received,
a moiety of the reward deserved, because of its

poor estimate of the great work done at that time by its servants. Well did Dr. Frank Gunsaulus say:

"Marcus Whitman was more to the ulterior Northwest than John Harvard has ever been to the Northeast of our common country."

Two names which shine brightest upon the pages of English history are Dr. Robert Livingstone and Dr. John McKenzie, both missionaries, and both poor men. Their eminent services were along much the same lines as those of Dr. Whitman— services to the whole people and the nation. Dr. McKenzie made three trips to London before he could persuade the English authorities to plant their flag over Bechuanaland, the flower and wealth of all South Africa. But how England and English people have ever since loved to do honor to both these noble men! Dr. Whitman, by his eminent and heroic service, laid the American people under as great a debt of gratitude, and I simply point to facts already narrated to sustain that position. Have the people of the United States done their simple duty to its noble martyrs?

The Benefits to the Indians

As to the benefits from the missionaries to the Indians themselves eternity alone will reveal how little or how much good was conferred. The

Cayuse was a trading tribe of Indians, and were almost as unscrupulous in their dealings as Wall Street is to-day. Dr. Whitman had hard uphill work in changing their customs. Yet many of the Cayuse became Christians. Old Istikus was a prince among Christian men, savage as he was. For sixteen years after the death of his loved friends, he regularly went to the door of his wigwam, rang the old mission bell, and invited all to come in to prayers. General Joel Barlow, who was one of the commissioners after the treaty of peace in 1855, to settle the Indians upon their reservations, says:

"I found forty-five Cayuse and one thousand Nez Perces who have kept up regular family worship, singing from the old hymn books, translated into their language by Mrs. Spalding. Many of them showed surprising evidences of piety."

The most successful of the missions, as far as good to the Indians was concerned, was doubtless that of Mr. and Mrs. Spalding among the Nez Perces. They were the friends and companions of Dr. and Mrs. Whitman on that long wedding journey over plains and mountains. They were pushed far out in the wilderness by the Hudson Bay Company in what is now eastern Washington, and the Spokane country near where the city of that name is located. They were gentle, kind, and self-sacrificing, and perhaps were fortunate in being so isolated. The Indians received them and their message kindly, and soon there were many sincere and earnest Christians among them. A small printing-press was sent them from Honolulu that had become insufficient for their work there. Mrs. Spalding translated the Book of Matthew, some psalms, hymns, and a few school books, into the Nez Perces language, and they printed them with their little hand-press. It is said that, now after sixty years have passed, they still have some of them that are carefully treasured relics. They have never engaged in wars, remain in the lands of their fathers, are farmers and stock raisers, have churches and schools, and are respected by their white neighbors. One little touch of nature lingers with them still, one will often see an Indian teepee or wigwam in the yard or some place near a comfortable house. Doubtless the father often goes there to smoke his pipe in peace and comfort. Mr. Spalding lived to be an old man, and told and wrote much of the early life of the missions.

In these chapters we have purposely avoided discussing the motives which led up to the massacre. There have been many charges not fully sustained, that have caused ill feeling and done harm. But it is undoubtedly true that Dr. Whitman's activity to help settle Oregon with Americans was the direct cause of the great disaster. Dr. McLoughlin was driven from office for no other reason than his kindness to the missionaries that made Whitman's ride possible. Just as certainly Dr. and Mrs. Whitman perished because they loved the flag and all it represented, and were brave enough to express it by heroic acts whose results would not be misunderstood by the enemies of the republic. There is good evidence that Dr. Whitman understood the perils of his mission before entering upon it, but in such a character fear played a small part when confronted by duty.

CHAPTER XI

The Memorials to Whitman. Why Delayed. Why the History was not Written Earlier. Whitman College the Grand Monument! Professor Harris Defines "History the window through which the soul looks down upon the past and reads its lessons."

IT is of great importance that history be written accurately, and is best when written at the time of action by reliable observers. But there is much history of great value which was not currently recorded. The Bible record is an instance of this. Take the history of the battles of the great Civil War as another illustration. General Sherman, president of "The Army of the Tennessee," in every annual meeting, long after the war, declared the papers read before the society, and those read before "The Loyal Legion," descriptions of skirmishes, campaigns, and battles of the great conflict, as of greater value to history than were even the official reports made at the time of action; they were the personal experiences of many participants; that they caught the very spirit of the time and events, and were reliable although written thirty and more years later.

There were many valid reasons why the history of the North Pacific states in pioneer days was left unwritten for many years. It was mos fortunate that when the subject first began tu receive attention so many of the pioneers were still living, and that so much of the history had been preserved by the Pioneer Association of Oregon, and by individual records and letters. The writer reached Oregon soon after the massacre at Waiilatpui. He was a teacher of the boys and girls of the first settlers, and had access to their homes soon after the execution of the five Indian leaders. The scene of the execution was not far distant from the school-house in the fir woods. Naturally it was a subject for discussion in every intelligent circle. I thus learned historic facts not from books of written history, but from men who were makers of the history.

Why the Writing was Delayed

In less than eight months after the massacre, gold was discovered in California and Oregon, and no other event so absorbed the attention of the population of the Pacific Coast or we might say of the whole United States. They thought of little else for ten years. During the same period, an Indian war following the Whitman massacre was in progress in Oregon. Before these excitements ceased, the political upheavals, beginning in 1856, culminated in 1860. Then followed the great struggle of the Civil War, when giants met in battle, and the very existence of the nation hung upon the success of the men behind the flag. After 1865, the starry flag floated from ocean to ocean, from the lakes to the Gulf, came the troublous period of reconstruction—railroad-building and money-making as never before witnessed in the Republic.

It is not at all strange that under such conditions, at least such history as was made by a poor country doctor and his noble, unselfish wife should have been for the time neglected. Who will say that it is too late to remember such? In every civilized land the historian's pen, the painter's brush, and the sculptor's art have been taxed to place upon the library shelves historical books, upon the walls paintings, and upon pedestals sculptured marble; thus commemorating the noble dead, their great names live again as educators of the people.

The Memorials to Whitman Few

After leaving Oregon, the writer did not return for forty-five years; in the interim were wondrous changes. The giant forests of firs had disappeared, while cities, towns, and country homes, and waving wheat-fields had taken their places. But as I stood at ''the Great Grave'' of the martyrs, it alone was undisturbed and unchanged, in all these years!

To the great credit of loyal pioneers of Oregon who knew Whitman and his work, upon the fiftieth anniversary of his death erected a stately marble column above the grave and secured five acres of ground about it, while the Christian people of Walla Walla built a little Memorial Mission Church at the place of the massacre.

In a previous chapter we noted the action of the American Board and the Presbyterian statue to Whitman upon the fiftieth anniversary of his death.

It is gratifying to observe these marked evidences of awakened interest in the long-neglected Oregonian hero. It is but the beginning, for the name and honor of Marcus Whitman will shine with new luster in the years to come.

The Grand Memorial is Whitman College

It needs no argument to convince intelligent readers, young or old, that to such a character as Whitman, a great institution of learning is the best and most appropriate memorial. While it is a constant reminder of a noble, unselfish, patriotic Christian life, it is also a blessing to the whole people within its reach, by building up intellectual and moral character in the young men and women of that land for which he gave his life.

The story of Whitman College, like the life of the man it commemorates, gives a lesson in faith.

Dr. Cushing Eells was the co-worker with Whitman, and perhaps knew the inner life of the man better than any other. After the massacre he was driven from his post, but returned to the Indian country as soon as it was opened to white people. He at once visited the tragic grounds at Waiilatpui. As he stood uncovered at the great grave of his beloved friends, he writes in his diary:

"I believe the power of the Highest came upon me, and I asked, What can I do to honor the memory of these Christian martyrs who did so much for the nation and humanity? I felt if Dr. Whitman could be consulted he would prefer a high school for the benefit of both sexes, rather than a monument of marble."

We must remember that at that time there were very few schools in the Pacific States above the grade of the ordinary country district school.

The subject impressed him, and as he thought and prayed, it came to him as his life work and duty, to build such a monument. In memory of his friend he laid the matter before his good wife, it met with her cordial approval; and then before the Congregational Council, and they enthusiastically in-

MEMORIAL HALL WHITMAN COLLEGE.

YOUNG MEN'S DORMITORY, WHITMAN COLLEGE.

dorsed the work, and in a closing minute said, "The Whitman Seminary is in memory of the noble deeds and great work of the late lamented Dr. Whitman and his noble wife."

Dr. Eells, like Whitman, was a very poor man. The people about them were poor. But they were rich in the kind of "Faith that removes mountains." To financiers of modern times who demand millions for schools the outlook for Whitman Seminary would not have been marked as "promising." Dr. Eells bought the great Whitman Mission farm from the American Board for one thousand dollars (on credit), and began work. He and his wife were then well along in years, but that did not count, and they had two sons of like mind who still live to tell the story. For six years he plowed, sowed, reaped, and preached a free Gospel up and down the valley; while the good wife made butter, raised chickens, spun and wove, and at the end of that time, they had accumulated six thousand dollars to start Whitman Seminary. The charter was granted, the foundations laid, and work begun. The time came, years later, when the seminary grew into a college, and Dr. Eells had such strong and able men to aid and advise him as Dr. Anderson, the first president, Dr. Atkinson, Dr. Lyman, Dr. Spalding, and many others. But the college, while it had from the outset a good reputation, was poor; there was no. endowment, and the young men and women to be educated were poor. Dr. Eells devoted his time and life energies to his task, but in spite of all they had to place a mortgage of thirteen thousand five hundred dollars upon the property. One has to read the story in Dr. Eells' diary to know it in its completeness. In its darkest days, when the faith of others was small, his was still as strong as at the beginning. The last entries in his diary, just before his death, were prayers for the upbuilding and full success of Whitman College.

The Story of Long Ago, and its Sequel

The sacred word says, "A word fitly spoken is like apples of gold in pictures of silver!" Who can overestimate the power of a good word or a good act? Drop a stone in the middle of a placid lake and the circles begin and widen until they reach the farthest shore. So with good words and good acts, they go on and on into the great future, in ways we know not of.

Congressman Thurston was a Maine man— a fine type physically, intellectually, and morally. He had early immigrated to Oregon, and was the first congressman from that territory. It was too far to return to Oregon for his summer vacation, over the slow routes of that day, so he went up to Chicopee, Massachusetts, to spend the summers of 1848 and 1849. The house where he boarded was one of the old-fashioned New England double houses, with a wide porch across the entire front. It so happened that a young doctor and his wife occupied the other side of the house, and the front portico was the common retreat in the long summer evenings. He loved to tell of the majestic forests of fir and pine trees, fifteen feet in diameter and three hundred feet high, of the grand rivers, rich soil, and its great future. It was not until 1848 that word reached the States of the tragic disaster at Waiilatpui, and the death of his dear friends, Dr. and Mrs. Whitman. The incidents and heroism of their lives were told by the eloquent, earnest congressman, in a way that made a deep and lasting impression upon the young doctor and his good wife. They were seriously casting about for some wider field in life, and were almost persuaded to make Oregon their future home. Upon the homeward journey to Oregon in 1850, Congressman Thurston lost his life in a great ocean disaster upon the Pacific. The writer was in Oregon at the time, and well remembers the wave of sorrow that spread throughout the territory. After the death of Thurston, the young doctor gave up the Far Western journey, but he still had "the western fever," removed to Illinois, and bought a small farm. Prospecting through that state, Wisconsin and Michigan, he made up his mind that there was money in pine land, and beginning in a small way, marketed the timber, and made money. He at once invested all his money in pine timberland, bought and sold, and ever bought more pine, and the time came when he could readily sell for four times the cost of it. He was an observant man, and his success in locating and selling, by his straightforward way of doing business, soon attracted the attention of capitalists, and they persuaded him to settle in Chicago and buy and sell for them. Soon an immense business was in his hands, which continued for years, and left him with a fortune. He wearied with the years of intense business activity, retired, and said to himself, here is a snug little fortune, what is to be done with it? In the language of a notable address, delivered by the doctor before a great audience at Battle Creek, when he said, "These dead hands can carry nothing out! What, gentlemen, are you going to do with your money?" He soon settled upon a plan to spend his, and that was to use it through deserving struggling Colleges, to give to poor young men and women an intellectual, moral, and religious training. He believed that every institution for its permanency and security should have a healthy, interested, money-giving constituency about it, and so he gave in a way to induce others to give, and aids no institution where the Bible and moral training are neglected. I scarcely need tell my intelligent readers this person is D. K. Pearsons, M.D., LL.D., of Chicago, now eighty-six years old.

I have given, in brief, a sketch of his work in this connection, first because of his direct association with it, and secondly, because it pointedly marks what we have tried to show from historic facts in all the chapters — that Power higher than man's power can be traced and studied.

We often speak of all such as "accidental happenings." *Were they?* Did the four Flathead chiefs accidentally, in 1831–32, appear in the streets of St. Louis upon their strange mission and there meet their old friend the great red-head chief? Were Drs. Whitman and Spalding and their wives accidentally in Oregon? Was his heroic ride to save Oregon in 1842 an accident? Was it accidental that he was on the border in 1843 to lead that great immigration to Oregon in safety? The Oregon of to-day was dependent upon the safety of that great company in 1843. Was it all accidental that Congressman Thurston met Dr. Pearsons in 1848–49 at Chicopee, Massachusetts, and by "words fitly spoken," that forty-five years after he had rested in his watery grave were found to be "apples of gold in pictures of silver"?

We all view such events from different standpoints, and I do not stop to argue, only to state facts historically accurate. There are accidents in the physical world from violated laws certainly, but in the moral uplift of the race there seems to be an invisible hand, and an agency greater than man's power. Wise as the race has grown, we cannot understand and explain the mysteries that surround us. I see the poor young Doctor in 1848 struggling to master his professional work, and I see him again in 1894, old and rich, and in January of that year, he sat musing by the fire in his winter home in Georgia, and he took his pen and wrote:

LITHIA SPRINGS, GEORGIA, January, 1894.
TO THE PRESIDENT OF WHITMAN COLLEGE, WALLA WALLA,
　　WASHINGTON:—
Dear Sir:
　I will give Whitman College fifty thousand dollars for endowment, provided friends of the College will raise one hundred and fifty thousand additional,
　　　　　　　　Yours,
　　　　　　　　D. K. PEARSONS.

Some may say "Nothing strange in that. Dr. Pearsons had made large gifts to thirty-four different colleges." That is true. I one day asked him, "Did any one ever ask that gift to Whitman College?" He replied, "No; no one asked me for a

REV. S. B. L. PENROSE, PRESIDENT OF WHITMAN COLLEGE

dollar, and the president of the college evidently
thought my proposition preposterous, for he never
even replied to my letter.'' It was in the dark
days of the college. President Eaton was a good
man, but he had lost the strong faith of his pre-
decessors, and soon after resigned. Just then
the Yale Band of Missionaries invaded Washington, and Rev. S. B. L. Penrose, a man of Eells
faith and Whitman's courage and perseverance,
was chosen president. He at once visited Dr.
Pearsons, thanked him for his generous offer, and
set about his task of raising the money. The difficulty was in getting a start. On June 20, 1895, the
book ''How Marcus Whitman Saved Oregon'' was
published in Chicago, and on the Fourth of July,
Sunday, two weeks later, forty ministers in Chicago
and neighboring places took Marcus Whitman as a
patriotic text. Many of them took up collections
for the memorial college, and the Congregational
Club gave its check for one thousand dollars. Vir-
ginia Dox, an eloquent and enthusiastic pleader,
took up the work, carrying it through Michigan,
along northern and central Ohio and all New England from Maine to Massachusetts, and the one
hundred and fifty thousand was raised, and the
Doctor's fifty thousand added. The Doctor, in
the meanwhile has paid off the mortgage debt of
thirteen thousand five hundred dollars. Every-

thing looked brighter. But the buildings were poor and over-crowded, the campus of five acres too small. It was a good fortune which enabled the directors to buy eighteen acres adjoining, and admirably adapted for the purpose.

Dr. Pearsons then said, "You need a dormitory for young men, where they can be cheaply and comfortably fed and housed, and I will give fifty thousand dollars to erect a memorial building to Dr. and Mrs. Whitman if others will erect the dormitory." Through the aid of Mrs. Billings of New York (the largest giver), Billings and Memorial halls went up simultaneously. Then Dr. Pearsons said, the girls need a dormitory as well as the boys, let others build it, and I will give fifty thousand to endowment. It was done.

The people of Walla Walla, though possessed of no surplus wealth, came nobly to the rescue and contributed several thousand dollars, and the poor professors and many students literally gave "all that they had, even all their living," in making up the required sum. And so it has been from the beginning a college built by faith and self-denial. It has still many great needs, but its friends still hope and believe that its wants will be supplied.

Some time ago the writer read the story of an orphan newsboy, a waif of the streets, but a manly little chap. He attended a mission Sunday school and became a Christian boy. Some weeks later, one of the smart young men half-sneeringly said to the boy, as he looked at his broken shoes and tattered garments, "Well, my boy, if I believed in God as you do, I would ask Him to tell some of those rich church people to give me some better shoes and nicer clothes." The little fellow looked troubled for a moment, and then replied, "I expect He did, but they forgot."

It was one of the great characteristics of the men and women of these pages, that they listened, heard, and never "forgot."

The world to-day, and in the generation to follow, is in need of strong men and noble women. Greater problems than the fathers have solved will the sons be called to solve. Be ready for them. Mistaken Christian teachers have sometimes used the words "Prepare to die." Change them to read "Prepare to live," and may you live long and bless the world by your living. In this land of ours, the poorest can aspire to and reach out for grand achievements. The poor, half-orphan boy, conning his lessons by a pine knot fire in his grandfather Whitman's old New England home, or as he went through his classical course, and the study of his profession, then learned to be a millwright, and learned all about machinery, perhaps never dreamed of the great work he was to be called to do. He simply did it all well! That is the key which unlocks the future good things of earth, and swings wide open the everlasting doors of the eternal world. You are here for work in a broad field, and while you toil, be happy, joyous, contented, and make others the same. The children of earth are in partnership with the Great Ruler of the universe in the moral government of this world. His great law is love. Love is the greatest word in the language. The Bible represents God's love, as "like a flowing river." Drink deep of it, as have our heroes and heroines, and when taps are sounded, whether in the quiet of your homes or amid the yells of savage men, as befell our loved ones, you can say with St. Paul, even when the feet of his murderers echoed from the walls of his dungeon, "I have fought a good fight, I have finished my course, I have kept the faith, thenceforth there is laid up for me a crown of righteousness." You can sing with Tennyson in his age:

> "Twilight and evening bell,
>   And after that the dark;
> And may there be no sadness of farewell
>   When I embark.

> "And though from out the bourne of Time and Place
>   The flood may bear me far,
> I hope to see my Pilot face to face
>   When I have crossed the bar."

THE END.

.

CPSIA information can be obtained at www.ICGtesting.com
Printed in the USA
BVOW03s1656070813

328043BV00001B/92/A